YOU <u>CAN</u> GET
YOUR REAL ESTATE
TAXES REDUCED

McGraw-Hill Books by the Author:

Real Estate Guidelines and Rules of Thumb
You <u>Can</u> Get Your Real Estate Taxes Reduced

YOU <u>CAN</u> GET YOUR REAL ESTATE TAXES REDUCED

Ronald E. Gettel MAI, CRE, SREA, ASA

McGraw-Hill Book Company

New York St. Louis San Francisco Auckland Bogotá Düsseldorf
Johannesburg London Madrid Mexico Montreal New Delhi
Panama Paris São Paulo Singapore Sydney Tokyo Toronto

A special acknowledgment is due the contribution of Patti L. Gettel, who suggested the first four words . . . and then helped with all the rest of the words.

Library of Congress Cataloging in Publication Data

Gettel, Ronald E, date.
    You can get your real estate taxes reduced.

    Includes index.
    1. Real property tax—United States—States.
2. Property tax credit—United States—States.
3. Taxation, Exemption from—United States—States.
I. Title.
HJ4181.G48   336.2'2'0973   76-23173
ISBN 0-07-023174-5

1234567890 KPKP 786543210987

The editors for this book were W. Hodson Mogan and Patricia A. Allen, the designer was Elliot Epstein, and the production supervisor was Teresa F. Leaden. It was set in Aster by Progressive Typographers.

Printed and bound by The Kingsport Press.

In memory of George H. Gettel
and E. Jane Gettel

Contents

Relief and Exemptions

Tangible Personal Property

It is a national outrage that in an age of computer technology, most governments fail to administer property taxes fairly.

SENATOR EDMUND S. MUSKIE

If what happens daily many times in the administration of the property tax were to happen in plain view on the street we would call it unarmed robbery.

RALPH NADER

. . . the real property tax, if properly administered, has not lost its value. It has fallen into disrepute because it has been so badly, unfairly, and frequently corruptly managed.

SENATOR CHARLES H. PERCY

YOU <u>CAN</u> GET
YOUR REAL ESTATE
TAXES REDUCED

Chapter 1

A Strange and Capricious Tax

Once upon a time, in a beautiful land by the sea, dwelt a very gentle people. The sun shone. The birds sang. Life was good.

But it was not perfect. For the gentle people labored under a strange and capricious tax on their properties. So capricious was this tax that some were made to pay five times their just shares while their neighbors paid little. Yet so gentle were the people that most of the afflicted simply grumbled, shook their heads, and went about their business.

Once upon a time is now. And that beautiful land is *our* land.

As you will see shortly, the real estate tax system is like a great big Rube Goldberg machine. It has way too many moving parts in relation to the job it is supposed to do. It whirs and swoops and grinds foolishly. The bystander shakes his head and wonders at the reverse ingenuity of it.

But the analogy breaks down. Rube Goldberg designed machines to amuse and entertain. But what is amusing about an unfair assessment? And what is entertaining about a system that is so opaque you may not even know you are being skewered?

When you receive a property tax bill, do you assume that

- The bill is fair if the tax value is below your property's market value? (This is what assessors *hope* you will assume. But it is *not* the definitive test.)

- Whoever valued your property was qualified to do so. (Most are not.)

- Your assessment was carefully prepared? (Most aren't.)

· The most reliable valuation methods were used? (It seldom happens.)

· You probably couldn't do anything about the assessment even if it is too high? (Oh, but you often *can*.)

· You can't get "special relief"? (Several types are available.)

If you would protect yourself from abuse and take advantage of opportunities for relief, you need to know something about how the system works, how to tell if a particular assessment is too high, how to get a too-high assessment reduced, and several other ways to save.

Read on, gentle reader, read on.

Chapter 2

ABC's of the Real Estate Tax

When the mystery is taken out of assessing—when each taxpayer is informed of the assessment on his property and how it relates both to other assessments and to the legal standard—the taxpayer will be in a position to evaluate the fairness of the tax.

—*Excerpt from a report by the Advisory Commission on Intergovernmental Relations*

HOW THE TAX IS ADMINISTERED

The worst-administered tax of all.

That's what some people say about the real estate tax. But it isn't accurate. Oh, the administration is atrocious all right, but there is no *one* real estate tax. There are 51 sets of laws—one for each state and one for the District of Columbia—and these laws differ from state to state. These 51 are subdivided into more than 13,000 separate property tax districts. And the laws are not applied uniformly from one of these districts to another.

The extent and the results of this crazy-quilt arrangement are incredible. These four quotes will give you some idea *how* incredible. According to Byron L. Drogan, State Tax Commissioner of North Dakota:

> North Dakota, a State with a population of 620,000 has nearly 1,800 property tax assessors. Of those 1,800 assessors, I would estimate that no more than 75 would pass a minimum qualification test for the position of property tax assessor if such an examination were mandatory.

Or Senator Lee Metcalf of Montana:

> Subcommittee research has found, for instance, that no Montana assessing agency has a qualified industrial appraiser on its

3

payroll, even though the assessed value of industrial sites and improvements in the State in 1970 totaled more than $160 million.

Or Kenneth M. Curtis, Governor of Maine:

Less than 1% of the 1,500 assessors are considered to be professionally qualified. . . . So, the inescapable conclusion is that Maine's largest and most significant tax system is being administered generally by untrained, part-time, amateurs in 496 separate assessment districts with little in the way of uniform standards or procedures.

Or Senator Charles H. Percy of Illinois:

According to the Advisory Commission on Intergovernmental Relations, Illinois has 1,424 property tax districts. The resulting Balkanization of taxing jurisdictions leads to many problems: Serious disparities among taxing districts, adverse effects on land use and planning and multiple opportunities for abuse of the tax itself.

HOW THE TAX WORKS

A key Latin phrase for those who would understand property taxes is *ad valorem*. Ad valorem means "according to value." In principle, property taxes are supposed to be ad valorem taxes; basically, the amount of tax is supposed to be based upon the value of the taxable property—and not upon who owns that property and not upon what that property is used for. In *practice*, however, there are many exceptions to this. Some are lawful exceptions. Some are not.

Even people who have paid property taxes for decades rarely have a clear understanding of how individual property tax burdens are figured. Understandably so. Terminology is often misleading. (For example, figures given labels like "true value" and "full value" are seldom either true or full.) Many exceptions are made to the ad valorem principle. And laws and procedures vary from one place to another.

However, the basic methods are really pretty simple, as you can see in the accompanying summary, "How Property Taxes Are Levied in the Village of Gad." If the Gad Assessor appraised Gad's three taxable properties *consistently*, then the resultant tax burdens fell fairly on the owners. (If the smaller house in Gad really *does* have a value equal to one-fifth of the value of all the taxable parcels in Gad, then the owner of that house should pay one-fifth of the property tax.) Assuming that none of the owners of Gad's taxable properties challenge the assessments or the tax bills, then these taxes become a lien on these properties. If the tax on any Gad property is not paid when due, a penalty amount is added to the bill. Then if the tax is still not paid within a required time, the Gad Valley Sheriff comes and holds a public sale of that property.

Of course, the Gad example is simplistic. Things do not work out that simply and neatly in *your* tax district. Whoever values your property doesn't value taxable properties consistently. Further, six states have classified property systems, which simply means that different assessment ratios are used for different classes of property. (For example, in Tennessee, properties of public utilities are supposed to be assessed at 55 percent of market value, commerical and industrial properties at 40 percent of market value, and farms and residential properties at 25 percent of market value.) Tax rates may be expressed in terms of so-many-dollars-and-cents per $100 of assessed valuation or as a mill rate (so much per $1,000 of assessed valuation). A very small percentage of assessments are appealed, and most of the appeals result in reductions. The tax bills of millions of Americans are also reduced because they are over a certain age, because they are disabled, because they have low incomes, because they have mortgages, and/or for other reasons.

WHO DECIDES THE TAXABLE VALUE?

Who decides what the value of a taxable property is? Initially, it's usually the local tax assessor who decides. And since there are currently something over eighty million taxable parcels in the United States, that's a lot of deciding. So let us take a look at who it is that is doing all of this deciding for us.

In most states, assessors are elected. Some are politically powerful. (According to Senator Percy of Illinois, when John F. Kennedy

HOW PROPERTY TAXES ARE LEVIED

In the mythical Village of Gad are four properties: two homes, a store, and a church.

Now the Gadites figure that they will need $2,000 from real estate taxes next year to help run the village. And here is how they go about getting the money:

1. First, the Gad Assessor estimates the full market value of each taxable parcel.

2. Next, the Gad Assessor converts the appraised values to assessed values. (Appraised value × assessment ratio = assessed value. In Gad's state, the law says that all taxable properties will be assessed at one-half of appraised value.)

3. Then, the Gad Clerk sets a tax rate:
   Tax to be collected ÷ all assessed values = tax rate
       $2,000   ÷ $50,000   = 0.04

4. Finally, the Gad Clerk prepares and mails the tax bills.

IN THE VILLAGE OF GAD

Appraised value:	$20,000	$30,000	$50,000	Exempt	$100,000
Assessment ratio:	×50%	×50%	×50%		×50%
Assessed value:	$10,000	$15,000	$25,000		$ 50,000
Tax rate:	×0.04	×0.04	×0.04		×0.04
Tax bills:	$ 400	$ 600	$ 1,000		$ 2,000

had a fund-raising dinner in Chicago, he ". . . publicly thanked the tax assessor of Cook County for selling such a large number of tables. Not that he was such an eloquent salesman . . .") Some are nearly impotent. (Jonathan Rowe of Ralph Nader's Tax Research Group said, "The State of New Jersey, for example, has over 500 local assessment units; I am told that in some of these units, if you want to find the assessor, you have to go down to the gas station where he is pumping gas during the day.")

Sixty percent of state governments have no explicit professional requirements whatsoever for the position of assessor. Requirements in several other states are meager. In terms of important professional qualifications, most new assessors come to their jobs *tabula rasa*. (Another bit of Latin. Loose translation: with nothing written on their blackboards.) A few eventually master their jobs. Most never do.

In *principle*, the property tax assessor's role is as simple as ABC:

A. Discover the taxable properties

B. List them

C. Value them

In *practice*, however, the job is usually not done well because of one or more of these problems:

1. Lack of expertise

2. Too-small staff and budget

3. Archaic laws and procedures

4. Political pressures

5. Press of other duties

6. Personal biases or mind-sets

7. Corruption

8. Inadequate state supervision

Because of their own lack of expertise and their limited resources, assessors often hire private "mass appraisal" firms to set values for them. How has *that* worked out? Listen to Clifford Allen, Metropolitan Assessor of Nashville and Davidson Counties, Tennessee:

> This deficiency in basic training and professional competence and skills is even more obvious among the thousands of low paid employees hired by certain mass appraisal firms, which hold themselves out to be "professionals," but whose work in many cases has been so shoddy and imcompetent as to constitute a racket and outright fraud upon the local taxpayers who become their victims.

Are the taxable "values" the assessors and others decide on really far out of line? Yes, *far* out of line. Said Alan C. Stauffer, Research Assistant of the Education Commission of the States, "Generally, what our study found was that the States have not taken the necessary steps to regulate the local assessor and to insure tax uniformity. For example, in our Louisiana tax district, property tax assessments ranged from 1 percent to 550 percent of market value."

HOW ABOUT DOING AWAY WITH REAL ESTATE TAXES?

Various people have been denouncing property taxes for fifty centuries.

"But despite its unpopularity, the property tax will not likely fade away. Nearly 85 percent of all local government tax revenues come from the property tax." So said Senator Muskie.

If local governments are to function more or less independently, where else are they likely to turn for more than fifty billion dollars each year? Much as we may resent property taxes, it seems that this judgment of Dr. Layton S. Thompson, Professor of Economics at Montana State University is a sound one:

> Some have suggested that we just replace the property tax with something else. Now if any of you take a pencil and a piece of paper and figure how much income tax you would have to have to replace the property tax, you will see that is a large order.

Nobody with good judgment I think is saying we can do away with the property tax. We don't need to do away with the property tax but we don't need to hit it for everything.

AREN'T THERE SOME GOOD ASSESSORS?

The author does not want to overstate the case. There are at work today some assessors and other property tax officials who are both well-trained and dedicated to the public interest; fine men and women who do not deserve to be lumped with the rest.

However, there are far too few of them, and even *they* are often not adequately supported. The 1973 president of the International Association of Assessing Officers (IAAO) said it well:

> . . . criticism of the property tax has long centered on inadequate administration by unqualified personnel. This argument is so prevalent that it is easy to forget that many, many jurisdictions have first rate assessment administrators, often struggling with a tremendous valuation task with little support from their government. However, too many governments rely on inexpert assessment administration. The property tax is simply too important to warrant such neglect . .

The same year, a survey of IAAO members revealed how *assessment officials themselves* view the quality of assessment administration in the country as a whole. Sixty-two percent of the respondents rated it as relatively poor.

ARE YOU SYMPATHETIC?

You may sympathize with the relatively few capable assessors. You may even sympathize with the thousands of inept ones. But you do not want to be just another of the millions of victims of this ugly system.

Chapter 3

A Very Short Course in How Properties Should Be Valued

You cannot have fair assessments unless the properties are valued fairly.

On the next four pages are two summaries of what's involved in appraising real estate.

Unfortunately, most assessors do not use sound valuation methods. Incomplete property inspections—often called "windshield" or "horseback" inspections because the property inspector may not even get out of his car to inspect some of the parcels—are still common. The cost approach is almost universally used to value improvements, often crudely developed and relied upon when it is unreliable. In many assessment jurisdictions, the other two approaches are not set out—*ever*. For example, here is what a study for the U.S. Department of Housing and Urban Renewal reported:

> Chicago . . . pays no attention to market value in its original assessment. The city follows a four-year neighborhood assessment cycle, but assessed valuations are determined on the basis of a structure's reproduction costs and depreciation. No attempt is made to make reassessments reflect changes in neighborhood property values or in the income generating possibilities of a structure, unless the assessment is appealed. At the time of the appeal, market value and net income are admitted as grounds for revising the assessed valuation. But the responsibility for introducing market considerations into the assessment procedure lies entirely with the owner.

ABC'S OF REAL

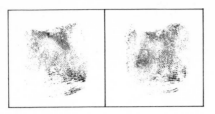

Each Parcel Is Unique.

As with fingerprints, no two parcels of real estate on this earth are exactly alike. That's one of the reasons we need many skilled appraisers. (If you want to know the value of one share of General Motors common stock, you can find out in minutes and at no cost. This is so easy because any one share is exactly equal to any other share.)

But Not Too Unique

Highly trained real estate appraisers can work with a unique commodity intelligently by using sound economic principles. Just one example is the principle of substitution: We know that the maximum value of a property tends to be set by the cost of an equally desirable (if somewhat different) substitute property, assuming that no costly delays are involved in the substitution. (An informed buyer normally won't pay $50,000 for a house if he can readily buy an equally appealing one in the same submarket for $40,000. Thus, a skilled appraiser valuing one parcel will normally study recent sales and current offerings of similar properties in the same submarket.) Basic economic principles adapted by appraisers include supply and demand, increasing and decreasing returns, anticipation, contribution, and several others.

What Kind of Value?

In most assignments, the appraiser is to estimate market value. Market value may be defined as the amount a property is most likely to bring if a reasonable time is allowed to find a purchaser, if both seller and buyer are fully informed, and if there are no abnormal influences. (Under abnormal influences, market *price* can be very different from market *value*.) However, an appraiser is sometimes called upon to estimate insurable value, or value in a particular use, or some other kind of value.

ESTATE APPRAISING

And When?

The value of any real property changes over time—sometimes dramatically—in response to many factors. That is why skilled appraisers always estimate value *as of a specific time.*

What Is Valued?

Appraisers need to know exactly which property rights are to be valued, and they need to become familiar with the physical factors and the location factors of each parcel of real estate.

What Methods Are Available?

In simplest terms, what the appraiser does is study what typical buyers and sellers are doing in the particular submarket and then estimate the most likely price the subject property would bring under certain circumstances. There are three basic approaches to the value estimate: the cost approach, the market data approach, and the income approach. (See the accompanying summary, "A Quick Look at the Three Approaches to Value.")

Which Method Is Best?

In each appraisal assignment, the responsible appraiser considers all three approaches unless there is inadequate data available or unless one or more of the approaches does not apply. (Examples: The income approach may have no sound application to the valuation of a fine single-family dwelling, and the cost approach may have no sound application to the valuation of a vacant site.) In most cases, the appraiser develops more than one approach and, therefore, more than one indication of value. These are *not* averaged in order to develop a final estimate of value. Rather, they are correlated into a final estimate by giving the most weight to the approach (or approaches) which, by reason of having the best data or for other reasons, was judged most reliable.

A QUICK LOOK AT THE THREE APPROACHES TO VALUE

Mr. Typical Goes to Market. And So Does His Appraiser.

To illustrate the three classic approaches to appraising a property, let us suppose that a typical prospective purchaser—we'll call him Mr. Typical—is considering buying an existing apartment building, the Venus Arms. Mr. Typical retains an appraiser to estimate the market value of the Venus Arms.

There are three basic ways that Mr. Typical (or any other prospective buyer) could weigh the value of the Venus Arms. These are the same three basic ways the appraiser will approach the value of the Venus Arms.

The Cost Approach.

Instead of buying the Venus Arms, Mr. Typical *could* buy a lot and build a similar new building.

Paralleling this, one of the approaches the appraiser considers is the cost approach. The method of the cost approach is to:

A. Estimate how much it would cost to reproduce the subject improvements on the effective date of the appraisal.

B. Deduct an estimate of accrued depreciation (the difference in value from that of a proper new structure) because of adverse physical factors, adverse design factors, and adverse location and market factors.

C. Add an estimate of land value. (Usually, site value is estimated from a study of recent sales and current offerings of similar sites.)

This can be a very helpful approach *if the accrued depreciation is limited*. It is seldom very reliable if accrued depreciation is very substantial as in the case of old improvements, those in poor condition, and/or those of improper design. Why? Partly this is because there is no tool native to the cost approach (that is, not borrowed from one of the other two approaches) which can be reliably used to measure some types of depreciation.

The Market Data Approach.

Another alternative open to Mr. Typical is to buy some other existing apartment building instead.

And paralleling *this,* another approach the appraiser considers is the market data approach. The method of the market data approach is to:

A. Study recent arm's-length sales and current offerings of similar properties. The appraiser must understand how typical buyers and sellers of such properties look at such investments, for it is *they*—and not appraisers—who make values.

B. Select those comparables which are most similar to and most suitable for detailed comparisons with the subject property. One can compare one whole property with another whole property. One can compare some types of properties on the basis of gross rent multipliers. (A gross rent multiplier is a figure expressing the relationship of a property's gross rent to its sale price or market value.) Or property comparisons can be made on the basis of some meaningful unit. (Examples: value per apartment, value per rentable room, value per square foot of gross area, and value per square foot of net rentable area.)

C. Develop indicators of the value of the subject property by (1) comparing each selected comparable *one at a time* with the subject property and (2) making adjustments in the (whole or unit price of that comparable to reflect important differences between it and the subject.

If enough good data are available, this approach is normally favored by skilled appraisers because it is so closely tied to what buyers and sellers are actually doing in the market.

The Income Approach.

If Mr. Typical buys the Venus Arms, he wants a return on his money commensurate with what other investments of this sort are bringing.

Here again, there is a parallel in what the appraiser does in the course of his work on the Venus Arms; the appraiser also uses the income approach to value. The method:

A. Project likely income and expenses for the subject property for the typical year in the near future. The appraiser deducts likely *property* expenses (such as utilities and maintenance) but, in most cases, does not deduct capital expenses (such as principal and interest payments and income taxes) or depreciation. (The former are usually the same for anyone who might own the property, but the latter are not.) The result of this work is a projection of the anticipated annual operating income before deductions for debt service or depreciation.

B. Next, the appraiser translates this amount into an estimate of the subject property's value. This is normally done by dividing the projected income by a rate called a "capitalization rate." Where does the capitalization rate come from? It is selected by the appraiser only after (1) studying capitalization rates reflected by recent sales of similar properties, (2) seeing what rates of return are available on other investments now, and (3) considering any particular advantages or disadvantages of investing in the subject property.

Assessors too often rely on arbitrary formulas, questionable rules of thumb, and more-or-less educated guesswork. It is not unusual for assessors to use tables based on unproven "rules" made up in the 1800s. And it is not unusual for the assessment on a property to remain unchanged for many years while the value of that property is changing substantially.

It costs more to make good appraisals than it does to make bad appraisals. However, after a point, the factors are extra-economic; some assessors are doing far better work than some other assessors who have better funding.

One of the aids that money can buy is a computer program that can store vast amounts of market data and bring them to bear in a consistent fashion. However, the involvement of computers is no guarantee of fair valuation; a computer program without a skilled appraiser directing it can produce ludicrous figures. (A favorite slogan of people who work with computers: GARBAGE IN, GARBAGE OUT.)

The summaries on the preceding pages are simplistic, but real estate appraising is complicated and demanding. It is not for beginners—*even elected or appointed beginners.*

Chapter 4

How to Tell if an Assessment Should Be Challenged

In a system where assessments are erratically determined or systematically biased, the possibility of remedy through the appeals procedure is extremely important.

—*Excerpt from a report to the U.S. Department of Housing and Urban Development by Arthur D. Little, Inc.*

Quite often, one can get an assessment reduced without making a formal appeal. But first you have to find the grounds for a reduction.

GROUNDS FOR REDUCTION

If an assessment is too high in any respect, grounds for reduction are usually found in the answer to one or more of these five questions, the first two of which merit your special attention:

1. *Did the assessor make mechanical errors?* Finding a mistake in a building size or in simple computations—and there seem to be lots of mistakes—can put you in line for a sizable reduction. Chapter 6 will tell you some of the things to look for.

2. *Is the assessment on your property out of line with assessments on similar properties in your area?* Now here is where you want to avoid making the mistake that so many assessors hope you will make—are *counting* on you to make.

   Timorous politicians figure they can fool the public by deliberately setting assessments below market value.

17

And, unfortunately, they *do* fool taxpayers much of the time; their deception *works*. If assessments are low, then the tax rate must be increased in order to collect any given amount of tax; the same amount of tax is collected, but taxpayers are deluded.

Well, don't *you* fall for it. The most important test of the fairness of your assessment is *not* its relation to market value. It is this: *Is it fair in relation to assessments on other properties in your area?* If you have farmland worth $800 per acre and your assessment is based on an "appraisal" of $600 per acre, you may think you are getting away with something and have no idea you may really be a victim. If nearby farmland comparable to yours is typically "appraised" at $200 per acre, *you are paying three times as much real estate tax as you should.*

Chapter 7 shows how to test the assessment on your property against those on other properties in your area.

3. *Is the assessor's work in accord with valuation guidelines he is supposed to follow?* Many assessors follow an official valuation manual issued by a state agency—or at least are *supposed* to unless they have a valid reason to depart from it. Copies of these manuals can usually be purchased from the state, but they can be rather opaque reading for the inexpert taxpayer (and, alas, for the inexpert assessor). In this area of review, advice from an expert can be particularly helpful. (Chapter 10 gives you counsel on selecting expert help.)

4. *Has the property been appraised for more than its market value?* If it has, techniques shown in later chapters should be helpful. Here again, since real estate appraising requires expertise, you may want expert counsel.

5. *Is the assessment on your property a legal one?* Perhaps part of the assessed property is supposed to be excluded from the property tax because of the type of property it is. Perhaps part is supposed to be exempted because of its ownership or use. If you have doubts, look up information in the Supplement for your state. Then check with local tax authorities in your area.

OPPORTUNITIES FOR APPEAL

Suppose you find substantial grounds for a reduction in your assessment. How do you go about asking for a reduction? Basically, there are two types of forums available to you:

1. *Informal Hearings.* Most reductions in assessments are achieved without an official complaint or formal hearing.

   Often, a taxpayer (or his representative) simply calls mechanical errors to the attention of the assessor (or an aide), and the assessor will agree to correct them and mail out a notice of the amended (reduced) assessment. Sometimes, glaring inequities can also be corrected this easily.

   In general, the assessor is more likely to agree to a reduction without a formal hearing (at which time, criticism of the assessor's work will be presented to others) if the merits of the taxpayer's case are simply and convincingly presented. Often, the help of a recognized expert at even this early stage can carry substantial weight.

   Some assessors will not give sincere cooperation at this stage. Even if you tactfully point out an obvious error that has resulted in an overassessment, the assessor may refuse to correct it without a review of the whole assessment process—during which the assessor may "just happen to find" a reason for an offsetting (upward) adjustment. If you have reason to believe you are dealing with an assessor of this sort, you may do better to bypass the informal talks and tell your story to a review board.

   If the time comes for a periodic updating of tax valuations in your district and a mass appraisal firm is hired to do the work for the assessor, your informal discussion of discrepancies in the new figures may be with a representative of that private firm rather than with the assessor, or it may be with both.

2. *Formal Hearings.* If you feel that your property tax assessment should be reduced, local law affords you an

opportunity to petition for review of the assessment. Often, local tax officials will even provide an application form for you to use in asking for this review.

Typically, if you are to challenge an assessment for a particular tax year, you must do so by a certain cutoff date if it is an existing assessment or, in the case of a revised assessment, within a certain period after the change.

If the decision by the local review board is not agreeable to you, you may have the opportunity to appeal to a review board at the state level. Then if *that* review board does not agree with your protest, you normally can appeal to a court to review the assessment. However, a reduction is usually granted by one (or both) of the review boards, and very few cases are taken to court.

In a way, it may be misleading to call the time—often a half-hour or an hour—spent before a review board as a *formal* hearing. The business conducted is very serious indeed, but the conduct is often rather informal, sometimes candid, sometimes cordial. As informal as a coffee-and-donuts break in the middle of an 8 A.M. appeal. As candid as a board member volunteering that they will do what they can but that political considerations may keep them from giving as much relief as they should. As cordial as compliments on an unusually good presentation.

The systems for reviewing assessments are sometimes criticized as biased against the taxpayer. However, it is the author's experience that, if you have clear-cut grounds for reduction, if you present your case well, and if you are determined to get a reduction, you usually *will*. Despite some problems, appeal systems often work well because of review board members who very much give a damn about justice.

TO APPEAL OR NOT TO APPEAL

Probably no more than one or two assessments out of every hundred are challenged before a review board.

Why so few?

Certainly, it's not because the appeals are not successful. The overwhelming majority of assessments that are appealed are reduced. In a study of property taxes in ten major United States cities, Arthur D. Little, Inc., reported this sample:

	Total no. of properties with appeals	Appealed but no change in assessment	Assessment reduced 10% or less	Assessment reduced more than 10%	Appeal unresolved
Homeowner	2	0	1	0	1
2–40 units	12	2	4	4	2
41+ units	56	11	15	18	12
Commercial	15	2	6	7	0
All properties	85	15	26	29	15

Of the appeals that had been resolved, four out of five were reduced. And as the ADL report noted, "Success on appeal was quite evenly distributed by investor size."

And certainly the reason there are so few appeals is not because there are so few objectionable assessments. There are *millions* of bad assessments.

Then why *are* there so few appeals?

Largely, it seems to be because (1) most taxpayers are simply not informed about the need to check up on their assessments, and (2) the potential for savings on a large-income property is usually more obvious than it is on a small parcel.

You see, most of the people who make use of the appeal procedures are large investors. Here is what ADL found:

	Number of properties	Number appealed	Percent appealed
Homeowner	45	2	4.4%
2–10 units	42	4	9.5
11–39 units	80	8	10.0
40–399 units	152	33	21.7
400+ units	71	23	32.4
Commercial	30	15	50.0
All properties	420	85	20.3

Large investors are more apt to study their assessments, and they can better afford to acquaint themselves with the appeal system and to retain experts to aid them.

However, even many real estate professionals and many owners of major income properties do not fully understand how to test the fairness of assessments. Add to this the millions of owners of dwellings and farms and other parcels who do not even check out the way their assessments are figured, and you have some idea of why there are so few challenges.

To appeal or not to appeal? The answer normally depends on these two factors: Do you have clear-cut grounds for a reduction in your assessment, and does the likely reduction in your tax burden justify the trouble and expense of pursuing it? Sometimes the answers to these two questions will be fairly obvious. Sometimes you will want expert help in answering them.

Chapter 5

Are the Assessor's Records Open to You?

When a taxpayer receives a property tax bill higher than last year's, he should know why. . . . Thus, taxpayers themselves must and can be the policemen of the local tax system. They can and should demand access to the records and the procedures by which they are taxed.

—Senator Charles H. Percy

In the case of income taxes, you must figure your own tax and show exactly how you did it. If Internal Revenue Service employees have questions about what you did, they are not likely to be too shy to ask for an accounting.

But it's just about the opposite with your real estate taxes. Government workers figure your tax burden "for you," and they send you a tax bill which tells you little more than how much you owe. If you want to find out how your assessment was figured, it is up to you to go in and check the assessor's records.

Assessors are obviously *public* employees, and most of their records are generally recognized as *public* records. But when you show up at your assessor's office asking to see the card on your own property and cards on certain other properties, you may not be received with great warmth.

The majority of assessors recognize that most of their records are public records and will let you look at them, with certain reasonable limitations. (For example, only a limited number of cards may be examined at a time, and no cards are to be removed from the office.)

However, there is a great deal of foot dragging about showing records in some offices, and a few assessors have flatly refused to

23

show them. This foot dragging can range from subtle to not-so-subtle gambits. Examples: "Why do you want to see them?" "You know, we don't usually show a record to anybody but the property owner." "We're shorthanded and working on a year-end report. Could you come back in a couple of weeks?" "Those cards are out of the file now. Somebody must be working on them."

In some offices, the availability of records is a selective matter; sadly, some people who "know their way around" in assessor's offices and those who will make a fuss are more likely to gain access to information than the typical, polite taxpayer. In one office, parts of the property data and parts of the assessment computation were covered up so the public couldn't see them. An aide advised that this was in conformity with a judicial decision. The author opined that this should not hold up if challenged. Then the aide confided that he had been directed by the assessor to show the covered-up information if anyone made a fuss.

A number of defenses have been offered for such tactics. "If a lot of people come in, we just don't have the staff to handle them." "Some people damage the cards." "Some people make a big thing out of every little blank that isn't filled in exactly right." "We're trying to give everybody a fair shake. If they think the assessment is too high, let them prove it with their *own* figures instead of finding fault with ours."

Consider this story of the making of an assessor:

> Ben Bashaw peaked in high school. Back in those days, he was "Blitz" Bashaw, slow in class but blindingly fast on the gridiron. "Blitz" Bashaw was very popular.

> After high school, Bashaw stayed in his home city and worked in a series of sales jobs in which his celebrity was a definite asset. ("Know who I bought a car from yesterday? Remember old Ben Bashaw—"Blitz" Bashaw?")

> Bashaw's celebrity faded over the years, but it still was enough to help him past his opponent when he ran for County Assessor last year.

> Bashaw didn't know an easement from a 2 × 4 (and worse, didn't really care), but he did know something about loyalty; his first act as assessor was to fire the former assessor's staff and hire people who had helped in his campaign.

At first, it was fun for Bashaw to come into his big, modern office in the City-County Building and greet people and talk about football and what-have-you. But after awhile, things began to go bad. It seemed like there was a new complaint or problem every time he came in. How *could* you explain all these mistakes? And how could you avoid making more and more mistakes with this inexperienced staff? It was *so damned embarrassing.*

Well, one day last week, Bashaw had had enough. He came into his tax-exempt office which cost the taxpayers $36.65 per square foot, sat down in his tax-exempt chair, settled his feet confortably on his tax-exempt desk, and ordered that, henceforth, taxpayers could not see the parts of "his" records that show how their assessments were figured.

If your assessor makes the same decision as Ben Bashaw—if you are refused a look at exactly how your assessment was figured—what will you do? Talk with your lawyer? Talk with a property tax specialist? Make a complaint to the local newspapers? Complain to the local review board? Complain to the state tax board? Contact the taxpayers research group in your area? Complain to the chairman of the assessor's political party? These are all possibilities.

By the way, Ben Bashaw is not a real person. ("Bashaw" is a generic term for a self-important official.) If some of you assessors found this story a little embarrassing because of similarities with your own situation, it *should* be embarrassing.

Chapter 6

First, Look for Mechanical Errors

Here is an interesting one. It is a notice of change in assessed valuation sent to a resident in the country which changes the assessment from $750 to more than $1.4 billion. Now such an outrageous error is easily remedied because of its magnitude. But what caused it? . . .

—Barry Greever of Ralph Nader's
Tax Reform Research Group

Almost everyone makes mistakes sometimes. I do. And so, I expect, gentle reader, do you.

But for holy-Toledo-will-you-look-at-that mistakes, and plenty of them, it's hard to beat the typical assessor's office.

The author has found the same building valued twice. The same parking lot improvements added in twice. The wrong number of stories. Frame construction called masonry construction. Absurd measurements. Simple computations off by several hundred percent. In a single project, the author found technical mistakes totaling over $2 million.

Some assessments are so shot through with appalling errors that it's hard to believe they are real. What better example than the letter on pages 28 and 29? This was an actual case.

One point is obvious: if you want to know if an assessment is fair or not, one of the first things you should do is go to the assessor's office and check the property record cards for mechanical errors.

1. Is the lot size stated accurately? (You may want to refer to your deed, abstract, or engineer's survey. Don't rely on dimensions in a drawing made in the assessor's office.)

2. Are the sizes of the improvements stated accurately?
   (Don't guess. *Measure.*)

3. Are the improvements described accurately?

4. Are all the other statements of fact correct?

5. Are all the arithmetic computations accurate? (Check *all*
   of them. Even if you don't agree with some of the cost
   factors or depreciation percentages—or don't understand them—check the math for mistakes.)

The assessment record cards used by one assessor may not be
just like those used by another, but most look something like the
sample on pages 30 and 31. Shown are the two sides of a single
card, filled in with a hypothetical example.

Mechanical errors in filling out these cards are sometimes made
by people who are skilled and earnest. They are more often made
by people who are in "up over their hubcaps" and by those who are
pressing to fill out too many cards in one day.

The quote at the beginning of this chapter is from testimony before a Senate subcommittee, which also included several examples
of how badly a private firm hired by assessors actually filled out
property record cards. In its internal procedural manual, this
same private firm advised its employees:

> (Note that in cases where the appellant's opinion of the value
> differs greatly from the appraised value, it is always advisable to
> immediately check the property record card for mechanical
> errors.)

Good advice—*for all of us.*

RONALD E. GETTEL

3322 n. washington rd.   fort wayne, indiana   432-2482   *appraiser/consultant*

January 18, 19██

████████████████
Attorney at Law

████████████████

Re: Real estate tax assessment
on apartment property known
as ████████████████

Dear ████████

It appears to me that:

1. There are whopping errors in building sizes. Measurements
around the outside of each building are accurate. However,
somehow the assessor missed the length of the open court in
the center of each building by (Are you ready for this?)
about 100'. The result: about 45% of each open courtyard is
assessed as building area.

2. Further, some unfinished building areas are assessed as finished areas. Unfinished, unheated storage rooms and open
staircases at the ends of these buildings are treated as finished areas.

3. The number of apartments is misstated. The assessor lists five
more apartments than there actually are. He states that all
are 2-bedroom units, while four are actually 1-bedroom units.

4. The assessor's estimate of the average finished area per unit
is more than 15% off. Since the estimate of the finished building area was about 19% too high, and the unit count was inac-
curate, it is hardly surprising that this figure is not close.

5. In using the "Apartment Pricing Schedule" in the State's ap-
    praisal manual, basic square foot factors were not chosen for
    the right type of construction. Although these buildings have
    wood joists, frame roof construction, and largely frame wall
    construction, unit prices were taken from columns under "Fire
    Resistant", not from columns under "Wood Joists".

6. The construction quality rating chosen by the assessor is prob-
    ably too high. One may cite some relatively modest design
    features (Example: ceiling construction dropped below stand-
    ard ceiling height to enclose ductwork) and several indications
    that construction and workmanship were not particularly good
    (Examples: numerous roof leaks, sagging soffit, breaking-up
    of balcony walkways, rusting of metalwork, prominent cracks
    in drywall). This may be further supported by quality-rating
    comparisons with examples set out in the State's appraisal man-
    ual and with other apartment projects nearby.

7. A 20% depreciation allowance was made for blacktop paving,
    but a 50% allowance is typical for this component. If neces-
    sary, numerous examples can be cited from assessment records
    on other apartment projects in this area.

Enclosed are summaries, photos, and sketches which demonstrate the fairness of a
much lower assessment.

I assume you will want to discuss this before the appeal.

Sincerely,

Ronald Gettel

Ronald E. Gettel, M.A.I.
C.R.E., S.R.E.A., A.S.A.

Encl.

cc: ████████

Page Two

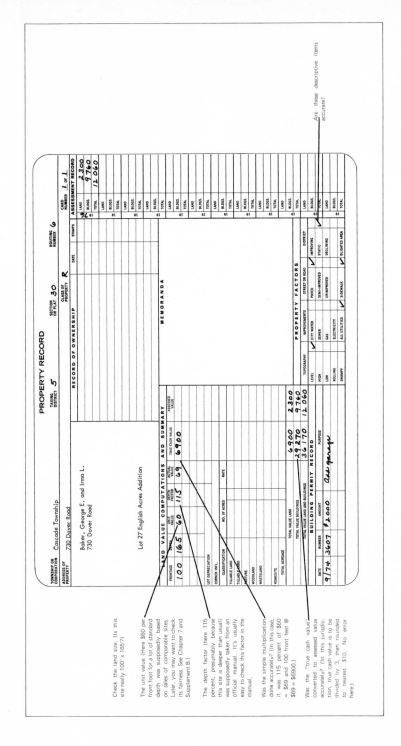

PROPERTY RECORD

TOWNSHIP OR CORPORATION: Cascade Township
ADDRESS OF PROPERTY: 730 Dover Road

Baker, George E. and Irma L.
730 Dover Road

Lot 27 English Acres Addition

TAXING DISTRICT: 5
SECTION OR PLAT: 30
CLASS OF PROPERTY: R
ROUTING NUMBER: 6
CARD NUMBER: 1 of 1

RECORD OF OWNERSHIP

DATE | STAMPS

MEMORANDA

LAND VALUE COMPUTATIONS AND SUMMARY

FRONTAGE	DEPTH	UNIT VALUE	DEPTH FACTOR	ACTUAL VALUE	TRUE CASH VALUE	ASSESSED VALUE
100	165	60	115	69	6900	6900

LOT DEPRECIATION
CORNER INFL.

CLASSIFICATION	RATE	NO. OF ACRES
TILLABLE LAND		
TILLABLE LAND		
PASTURE		
WOODLAND		
WASTELAND		
HOMESITE		
TOTAL ACREAGE		

TOTAL VALUE LAND	6900
TOTAL VALUE BUILDINGS	29 270
TOTAL VALUE LAND AND BUILDINGS	36 170

BUILDING PERMIT RECORD

DATE	NUMBER	AMOUNT	PURPOSE
9/74	3607	$2,000	Garage

PROPERTY FACTORS

TOPOGRAPHY	IMPROVEMENTS	STREET OR ROAD	DISTRICT
LEVEL	CITY WATER	PAVED ✓	IMPROVING ✓
HIGH	SEWER	SEMI-IMPROVED	STATIC
LOW	GAS	UNIMPROVED	DECLINING
ROLLING	ELECTRICITY	SIDEWALK ✓	
SWAMPY	ALL UTILITIES ✓		BLIGHTED AREA

ASSESSMENT RECORD

	'76			'61			'61			'61			'61	
LAND	2300													
BLDGS.	9760													
TOTAL	12 060													

Check the land size. (Is this site really 100' x 165'?)

The unit value (Here $60 per front foot for a lot of standard depth was supposedly based on sales of comparable sites. Later, you may want to check its fairness. See Chapter 7 and Supplement B.)

The depth factor (here 115 percent, presumably because this site is deeper than usual) was supposedly taken from an official manual. It's usually easy to check this factor in the manual.

Was the simple multiplication done accurately? (In this case, it was 115 percent of $60 = $69 and 100 front feet @ $69 = $6900.)

Was the "true cash value" converted to assessed value accurately? (In this jurisdiction, true cash value is to be divided by 3, then rounded to nearest $10. No error here.)

Are these descriptive items accurate?

30

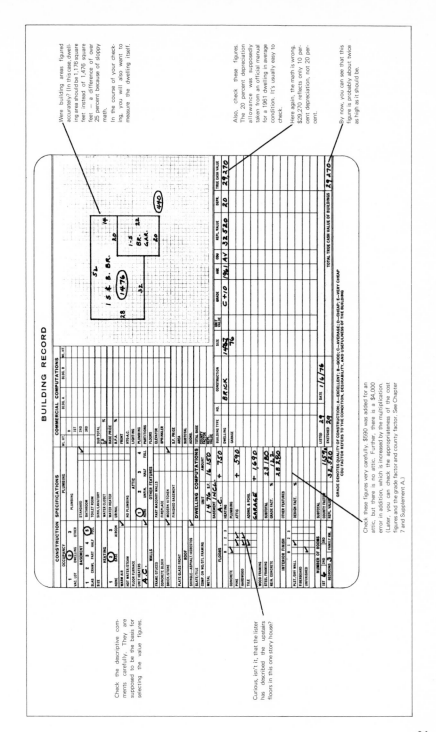

Were building areas figured accurately? (In this case, dwelling area should be 1,176 square feet instead of 1,476 square feet — a difference of over 25 percent because of sloppy math.

In the course of your checking, you will also want to measure the dwelling itself.

Also, check these figures. The 20 percent depreciation allowance was supposedly taken from an official manual for a 1961 dwelling in average condition. It's usually easy to check.

Here again, the math is wrong. $29,270 reflects only 10 percent depreciation, not 20 percent.

By now, you can see that this figure is probably about twice as high as it should be.

Check the descriptive comments carefully. They are supposed to be the basis for selecting the value figures.

Curious, isn't it, that the lister has described the upstairs floors in this one story house?

Check these figures very carefully. $500 was added for an attic, but there is no attic. Further, there is a $4,000 error in addition, which is increased by the multiplication. (Later, you can check the appropriateness of the cost figures and the grade factor and county factor. See Chapter 7 and Supplement A.)

31

How to Use Assessment Comparables

Homes of equal market value are often assessed at quite different values. Thus, two individuals with the same income and the same value home in the same jurisdiction may pay considerably different valuations by the local assessors.

—Wendell R. Anderson,
Governor of Minnesota

It is not important if the assessment be high or low provided it is uniform.

—Supreme Court of Virginia

Is your assessment reasonably consistent with assessments on similar properties? This is often *the* most important test of the fairness of an assessment.

Unfortunately, study after study has shown that similar properties are generally *not* treated uniformly. Not even close. You may be paying half as much as you should—but then again, you may be paying twice as much as you should.

One thing this means is that you had better be on your guard. Suppose your property is assessed at 60 percent of its market value. Are you going to accept this as fair simply because it is less than market value? Not if similar properties are typically assessed at 30 percent of market value; the assessment on your property would be much less than market value *but twice as high as it should be.*

In checking the fairness of your assessment, you may want to use what is often the most convincing test of all: Compare the way your assessment was figured with the way assessments were figured on the most comparable properties in your area. The approach is this simple:

1. Make a list of the properties in your area most closely comparable to yours. (Some of the best comparables may be right in the same neighborhood.)

2. Go to the assessor's office (sometimes the properties will lie in more than one assessment district), ask to see the assessment cards, and pencil out a side-by-side listing of important figures for your property and the comparable properties.

3. Compare these figures to see if your assessment appears reasonably in line with the others.

An example of this method is set out in the accompanying summary, "How the Assessment on This Dwelling Compares with Others." This sample happens to involve one type of property, but the method is applicable to all other types of property as well. Another example of this method—perhaps a better one—is provided for you in Chapter 12.

Assessments are sometimes successfully challenged without any discussion at all of market value—or of the three approaches to value. (And, for the most part, that's what is illustrated for you in the sample presentation in Chapter 12.) It can be enough to simply show that your assessment is out of line with (too high to be consistent with) those on similar properties.

However, it is not enough to show that your assessment is excessive as compared with those on only one or two other properties. Rather, one should show quite plainly that the assessment is out of line with the *typical* assessments in the taxing area. Here is an actual case that illustrates the point:

> A resident of a village in Minnesota didn't sit still for it when the village assessor raised the taxable valuation on his home by 62.7 percent. The heart of his appeal board was that the assessor did not raise the valuations on properties belonging to the mayor and a councilman and that his own valuation was now out of line with theirs. He won some points: his valuation was reduced, and the properties of the mayor and the councilman were revalued. However, there were indications that he might have done even much better if he had also shown that the assessment on his home was out of line with *typical* assessments on similar properties in the area.

HOW THE ASSESSMENT ON THIS DWELLING COMPARES WITH OTHERS

Selected Items in the Assessment on the Subject Property Compared with Those on Similar Dwellings (All Trilevels Built Since 1965) in the Same Neighborhood.

Location of comparable dwelling	Grade factor	Square foot cost (assigned to dwelling)	Depreciation allowed	Land valuation per front foot
317 Windsor Drive	C	$10.35	20%	$40
325 Windsor Drive	C	10.65	20	40
452 Windsor Drive	C+5	11.35	20	40
1723 Robinwood Court	C	10.35	25	45
1747 Robinwood Court	C−5	9.85	25	45
1753 Robinwood Court	C	10.65	25	45
1760 Robinwood Court	C	10.65	25	45
340 Dover Road	C	10.35	20	40
346 Dover Road	C	10.65	20	35
417 Lawton Circle	C	10.15	25	40
420 Lawton Circle	C	10.65	25	40
443 Lawton Circle	C+5	11.35	25	40
SUBJECT	B+5	$15.25	10%	$60

Regardless of their relationship to market value, assessments should be figured in a uniform fashion. If they are not, some property owners will be paying much more than their fair share, others less.

Sometimes, officials try to intimidate taxpayers complaining about *uneven* assessments by asking the taxpayers if they would like to sell their properties at the assessed valuations. Any official who uses this tactic may be

1. ignorant of the way property taxes are levied.

2. showing off.

3. a scoundrel.

4. all of the above.

Chapter 8

How to Show That Building Cost Does Not Necessarily Equal Value

Some assessors and other tax officials tend to feel that the building cost is a pretty fair gauge of a building's value. Sometimes it is not, but how do you make them understand this?

It may not be easy. If a building burns down, it's a simple matter to get the assessment lowered. But if a building "burns down" functionally or economically, that's often a different story.

Sometimes even brand new improvements are worth much less than their construction cost. Because of ill-conceived design, inefficiency, excessive competition in a particular submarket, shifts in demand, or some combination of these factors, a developer may spend much more than the completed property is worth. This can be disastrous enough. However, too often an assessor delivers a further body blow in the form of a too-high assessment based upon a myopic version of the cost approach.

As we saw earlier, most assessors are preoccupied with cost, cost, cost. They become reasonably comfortable with a simplistic version of the cost approach but develop little or no command of the income and market data approaches. A natural concomitant of this is a kind of reflexive feeling that COST EQUALS VALUE. Or at least that ". . . cost is pretty close to value unless you can prove to me that it isn't." Depreciation, when it *is* deducted, usually is taken from a mindless table that, at best, suggests *average* depreciation for a given age and condition.

Thus, when appearing before a review board, it is often necessary to discredit the COST-EQUALS-VALUE mind-set. How might you go about this? To illustrate some of the ways this might be done, imagine that *you* are addressing a review board right now and you need to make this point.

You might use a true story effectively (and this sample presentation *is* based on a true story):

YOU   It's so easy for all of us to fall into the trap of thinking that if something cost such-and-such, it's a pretty good bet that it's worth such-and-such. Cost *is* one guide to value, but every so often something happens to show us what a terrible guide cost can be if we follow it blindly.

Not long ago, a trial was held in Lake City because a redevelopment agency was acquiring a small vacant lot, and the owner wanted more money for it. This was not a pretty neighborhood. Some nearby parcels were deeded to the county because nobody would pay the real estate taxes. Others were just abandoned. Two experts called by the redevelopment agency testified that the vacant lot was worth several hundred dollars. The lot owner had no expert witness, and he had no lawyer, so he took the stand himself, and the judge helped him out. Here's how the transcript goes:

LOT OWNER.   . . . we are not even getting not even one-tenth of the money back.

THE COURT.   . . . Do you want to tell us what it cost you . . ., what you paid for it?

LOT OWNER.   What it costs us to tear it down, to take care of all the back property and everything, it costs us $4,500 and this is a ridiculous price to offer us $350.

THE COURT.   To tear what down?

LOT OWNER.   To tear the house down.

THE COURT.   Oh, are you saying there was a house on this lot?

LOT OWNER.   Yes, there was, and it could have been refixed up if it hadn't of been for the Health Department . . .

THE COURT.   When was it torn down . . .?

LOT OWNER.   It was tore down in '71. [Several years before the trial.]

THE COURT.   Is it your primary objection to this whole proceedings that it cost you that much to tear it down?

LOT OWNER.   Yes, because we had a fire. We was tearing it down ourselves and we had a fire and it costs us extra

money because it burned two other people's
home . . .

Well, the judge gave a generous verdict, but it was just a fraction
of the cost basis.

We are concerned with a different sort of property here this
morning, but a lot of money was lost in *this* case too. And I am con-
fident that the "judges" in this case will also be able to see the difference between cost and value.

Or, perhaps you would rather use an analogy:

YOU.   In this area, people rarely build houses over two stories
high. Just for a moment, let's suppose that a builder who
didn't recognize this put up a five-story walk-up house here,
found that nobody wanted it even at a deep discount, and
moved into it himself. Now if that unfortunate builder came
to you and said that he felt the value of his house was a great
deal less than the building cost, you would agree with him,
wouldn't you?

Well, *economically speaking,* the subject building is a five-
story walk-up. It is the Edsel of apartment buildings.

As you will see, the loss in value because of unfortunate
design is just as real as . . .

Or, you might prefer to use facts in the subject case itself:

YOU.   For thirty years, Gideon Ross has given the Bay Area some of
its proudest homes. His name is so synonymous with quality
that houses he built twenty years ago are often advertised
for resale today as "Ross-built" houses. His reputation for
excellence in homebuilding is of a special order in this area.

Unfortunately, in a way it was this very dedication to
uncommon quality, this habit of excellence, that set Mr.
Ross up for a very painfull fall. Two years ago, he decided to
build his first apartment project, and the result was something of a classic in terms of overbuilding. The carpeting
was of the same quality he had been putting into some of his
most prestigious homes. So were the appliances. There were
twice as many wall breaks as needed. An estimated $300,000

could have been pared off the building costs without even affecting the rent schedule.

Further, demand for high-rent apartments in this area has been very weak, and . . .

Often this sort of appeal is needed for a large development which is in trouble because the design is not in step with the market. And large developers who are in trouble should get the same treatment as anyone else in trouble. It's not supposed to matter who owns the property—it *is* supposed to be an ad valorem tax—but it too often *does* matter. An actual colloquy went something like this:

ASSESSMENT OFFICER.   Boy, you really almost had them in tears at the appeal yesterday! After you left, I had to talk till I was blue in the face to keep them from giving the *whole* store away.

REAL ESTATE SPECIALIST.   Did you believe what I told them?

ASSESSMENT OFFICER.   Well . . . yes.

REAL ESTATE SPECIALIST.   Then why did you feel like you had to try to keep them from approving what I recommended?

ASSESSMENT OFFICER.   Well, I think the developer's a big boy and ought to know better.

REAL ESTATE SPECIALIST.   Is that what you'll say about your children if *they* get in trouble?

Chapter 9

Be Aware of These Mind-Sets of Tax Officials

By law nominal tax rates are uniform within each jurisdiction. As a result of administrative caprice, corruption, intent or inefficiency, variations in assessment rates cause some taxpayers to face effective property tax rates many times those borne by others.

—Henry Aaron,
economics professor

The decisions made by assessors and other tax officials are often unlawful.

There are several reasons for this. Among the most important are personal mind-sets, attitudes, or biases which radically affect the way property taxes are administered in this country.

In this chapter, we will look at three of the most common types of bias.

WHO SHOULD PAY THE MOST TAX?

Only six states have classified property laws; in all the rest, all classes of property—dwellings, farms, apartments, stores, and the rest—are *required by law* to be assessed at uniform percentages of market value.

But it seldom works out that way. In countless districts there is a systematic bias in favor of certain classes of property, letting other classes take up the slack. To circumvent the law is a simple matter; just value different classes at different levels in relation to market value. And, in some districts, the extent of this favoritism by class is awesome.

In some areas, assessors tend to favor income properties. This

40

may be because large investors are more influential, are more likely to check assessments thoroughly, and may make sizable political contributions. It may be because the assessors feel more inadequate to deal with income properties. There may be other reasons.

However, systematic bias in favor of single-family dwellings and farms is probably more common. Said John Shannon, Assistant Director of the Advisory Commission on Intergovernmental Relations:

> The idea that the big boys are getting away with murder, and the low-income people and the homeowners are being overassessed in relation to income-producing property simply is not supported by evidence that is coming out of many of the central cities. There is a deliberate policy in many, many of our large cities, extra legal policy to assess homeowners at a lower percentage of the current market value than income-producing property . . .

> Now, if you take the hard assessment line that all property should be assessed at the same percentage of current market value, you will find in many of the largest cities that the property taxes are going to go up for the residential taxpayers and they are going to go down for the income-producing property. Now, according to law, that is the way it should be, and maybe that is the way you have to force it. But, the initial assumption that assessment reform will generally work in favor of the small homeowner and against the large property owner is not borne out by the evidence that we have seen.

Looking at it just a little differently, an assessor may depart from the ad valorem principle and try to vary assessments somewhat from class to class in terms of what that assessor perceives as *ability to pay*. Byron L. Drogan, State Tax Commissioner of North Dakota, described it this way:

> Generally speaking, the assessments are not good quality professional assessments particularly when you get out of the cities. Generally, small businesses are assessed on the ability to pay theory. North Dakota does not have a classification law. Landowners are generally assessed on a lower assessment ratio than is the residential homeowner. Likewise, the man on Main Street, the man who runs the Red Owl store, the Gamble's or any store,

he is assessed a little higher, because he is a businessman and the small town businessman is always considered the well heeled man. That flaunts the law in a sense.

Some people might liken one of these assessors to Robin Hood—taking from the rich and giving to the poor. Others suspect less lofty motives. (A political creature wanting to remain in office can be attracted to the notion of overassessing one shopping center by a million dollars and then underassessing a thousand homes by a thousand dollars each. On the other hand, if the shopping center owners are heavy political contributers, maybe . . .) They see something ugly and threatening in letting public officials make *personal* decisions as to who should pay how much.

Perhaps some types of properties *should* be favored. But, if that is what the *people* want, wouldn't it be better to do so legally and consistently rather than illegally and capriciously? After all, it is perfectly possible to make real estate tax relief a matter of law; in fact, every state now has laws giving relief to one or more of the following groups: governmental, religious and charitable, low income and the elderly, blind, disabled, veterans, owners of certain farms and open tracts, those with mortgage loans, and those who make certain types of improvements. So do some cities and other entities. So why is it necessary—indeed even tolerable—for many assessors to operate illegally?

What can you do if you feel your assessment is too high because of such bias? Techniques shown in this book can be adapted to show inequities *between classes of properties* just as clearly as they show inequities between individual properties of the same class. Arbitrary treatment of classes can be, and has been, challenged and beaten.

DO APARTMENTS PAY THEIR FAIR SHARE?

People who reside in single-family dwellings of limited value tend to pay limited property taxes. No assessor we know objects to that. Then why is it that so many seem to feel that people who live in apartments are not paying their share?

Now either the property tax is based upon the *value of the taxable property*, or it's not. If some people opt to live in apartments of limited market value, why should that form of economy frustrate an assessor any more than, say, people opting to make do with a less costly auto (also subject to property tax in many states)? It *is* an ad valorem tax, but you might not think so in some districts if you are challenging an overassessment on apartments.

What can you do if you encounter this bias? Partly, of course, the answer depends on the background of the person or group to whom you are appealing. Citing an authoritative study may help. (A good example: *"The Costs of Sprawl*, commissioned by three federal agencies and prepared by Real Estate Research Corp., reports that subdivisions of detached single-family dwellings cost their communities more in services, generate more pollution, and use more energy than higher-density developments.") Pointing out marked differences between a particular apartment project and some well-known subdivision of detached dwellings in the area can help. (Example: "Apartment units are not closely comparable to detached dwellings, but since you raised the question about the relative tax burden, let's look a little deeper. The tax revenue per apartment in Colonial Square is much less than the tax revenue from the typical home in Riverside Knolls. It *should* be. The largest apartment in Colonial Square has 970 square feet. The average house in Riverside Knolls is about *twice* that size. In Colonial Square, there are seventeen units per acre. In Riverside Knolls, the amount of land per unit is over *four times* as large. These big differences, and others, mean not only a lot more value per unit but also a lot more children to educate; a lot more streets, curbs, walks and sewer lines to maintain; and a lot more of other costs.") Above all, one must tactfully *insist* that the basic principle of property taxes, the ad valorem principle, be adhered to.

Expert real estate counselors now have some fairly sophisticated formulary to measure the fairness of the tax burden on single-family dwellings as compared with the burden borne by multiple-dwelling units. However, their use is usually not indicated in routine cases.

YES, BUT WOULDN'T THIS REDUCTION ENCOURAGE OTHERS TO APPEAL?

Suppose you own a downtown parcel, and you have just shown your assessor clear-cut evidence that the tax valuation is 55 percent higher than market value. This assessor has a reputation for being open-minded and sincere. Then why the foot dragging and wavering? Because the assessor is thinking this: "Every lot for three blocks along Main Street was assessed by exactly the same formula. If I make a reduction here, am I going to have twenty more owners around my neck? And If I lower land values along Main, then will the owners along Second start coming in?"

Understandably, assessors and members of review boards are often concerned about touching off a chain reaction. A sort of domino effect. If we make *this* reduction, will it bring a flock of owners of like properties scurrying in to file appeals?

If in seeking a reduction you encounter this problem, what can you do? Here are some alternatives:

1. Try to make your case so compelling that the assessor or the review board will make the reduction despite this concern.

2. Agree to a different form of reduction. For example, maybe it's the land that's overassessed, but the assessor or review board might prefer to reduce the assessment on the improvements or to make an unexplained reduction for economic obsolescence.

3. Join with other owners of like properties for a combined appeal effort. In one form or another, this has often been successful in combatting overassessments on one class of property or on parcels in a particular neighborhood.

Chapter 10

Do You Need Expert Help?

Many property owners are able to challenge assessments—and do so successfully—without help from experts.

Many others—even including lawyers, developers, and large corporations with considerable expertise—prefer to have some help from specialists. Some have specialists check out every real estate tax bill and every change in assessed value.

Independent experts have several advantages.

The most important of these is expert knowledge. Knowledge of the appraisal process. Knowledge of recent sales, rentals, and market trends. Knowledge of the procedures the assessors *should* be using and knowledge of the procedures they *are* using. Knowledge of what review boards have been doing in similar cases.

Other advantages may include a more impartial approach to the problem, easier access to certain types of data, and more experience in making such challenges.

There are more than 30 different professional designations in the real estate field. Some require much training and experience. Others don't. Even a real estate professional with very impressive credentials may not really understand the real estate tax system. Some of the most able experts are forbidden, or at least discouraged, by their professional societies from accepting such work on a contingent-fee basis. They charge by the hour or by the day, and the fee is not contingent on the outcome of the work. (Reputable professionals usually want the client to know the approximate amount of the fee at the outset. A common arrangement is a flat fee for a preliminary review of an assessment. The specialist reports to the client on the fairness of the assessment and on any grounds for reduction. Then, if the client is interested in retaining the specialist for further work, the two may agree on an additional fee.

In most sizable cities, there are firms that will undertake to get real estate taxes reduced *for a percentage of the savings.* The contingent fee arrangements vary, but a common fee is the amount of tax saved in one year. The principal appeal of this kind of arrangement is that you pay only for results. However, there are some cautions here too:

1. Assessors and appeal boards may doubt the sincerity of someone who stands to get a percentage of the reduction.

2. These people sometimes appear so often that they lose some of their effectiveness.

3. They often have skimpy credentials.

4. Many will not take small cases because the potential fee is too small.

5. If the reduction is a very large one, then the fee may be very large—perhaps much larger than the fee for a specialist whose fee is based on an hourly or daily rate.

Choosing such a specialist if you need one is a little like choosing a doctor. There is no simple criterion that one can rely on absolutely. The best approach is usually the same in both cases: Seek the advice of knowledgeable people in the field. Talk with your attorney, your banker, your accountant, any real estate professionals you know, any property owners who have retained experts, and others.

Chapter 11

How to Appeal More Effectively

The way to be a bore . . . is to say everything.

—Voltaire

Simplify, simplify.

—Thoreau

Truth is always the strongest argument.

—Sophocles

Here are ten guidelines for a winning appeal. (They are couched for a formal appeal, but most are good suggestions for informal appeals as well.)

1. Do not challenge any assessment unless there are *clear* grounds for reduction . . .

2. . . . and unless you are going to be thoroughly prepared to do so *properly*.

3. Tell the truth . . .

4. . . . but not the *whole* truth. (Limit your presentation to a few telling points. Do not try to "cover everything." It's hard to resist it, but *resist* it. Use less than the allotted time.)

5. Use visual aids. (Work on them until they will almost tell the story alone.)

6. Save your listeners the trouble of making notes by summarizing important points in writing and taking along enough copies for everyone who will hear the appeal. (Sometimes weeks will pass between your appeal presentation and the final decision, so this summary can be extremely important. Make it as persuasive as you can.)

7. Dramatics and humor do have a place in real estate tax appeals, but it's a limited place. (Bringing in real cannons for the *1812 Overture* usually excites concertgoers, but it may take their minds off the music.)

8. When you can do so honestly, agree with much of what the assessor did and stress that you do not question the assessor's sincerity. (Remember that an appeal is often perceived not just as a disagreement with the assessor's figures in one particular case, but also as criticism of the assessor. However, sometimes an assessor's work is so ludicrous or the assessor so hostile that this isn't possible.)

9. Be considerate of your audience. (Keep your presentation easy to follow. Be alert for signs of their interest—or lack of it. Encourage them to ask questions or make comments. Stick to the subject. Don't agrue or complain about real estate taxes in general.)

10. Make brief, clear recommendations on what the assessment *should* be. (Don't just show that the present assessment is improper. Show what it should be and why.)

An actual presentation is set out for you, starting on the next page.

Chapter 12

How One Actual Appeal Was Presented

Prolog: In the following presentation, two people show a tax review board why an assessment should be lowered—by two-thirds.

This example was chosen because it illustrates several points clearly. It happens to concern a golf course, but the basic methods can be used for all sorts of real estate. This presentation is not held up here as some great classic; rather, it is offered as an example of sound and effective work to get a too-high assessment reduced.

In June 1974, a new privately owned 18-hole golf course was opened for public play. In July, the developers were notified that the assessor had increased the "true value" on most of the land from just a few hundred dollars per acre to $3,500 per acre. The developers consulted their attorney and appraiser, who advised that the assessment was clearly excessive. The developers asked them to challenge it.

This is not a hypothetical case; it actually happened. No transcript of the presentation was made. No doubt the following "script" varies from what was actually said because the author has imperfect memory and a concern here for brevity and style, but it is believed to fairly represent what was said. The names have been changed, but the numbers are exactly as presented.

Presentation:

CHAIRPERSON.   Good morning. Has everyone met everyone else? Good. Let's see, we are concerned here with key number eight-zero-zero-ten, which is the Willow Creek Golf Course, isn't it? If everyone is ready (*inclining his head toward the attorney*), I think we can proceed.

49

ATTORNEY.

(*Standing*) Thank You.

It *is* the Willow Creek Golf Course parcel that we want to talk with you about for a little while this morning—or, more precisely, a 118-acre parcel that includes most of the Willow Creek acreage. Right now, there is only a limited partial assessment on buildings. The buildings may have to be dealt with later, but today we want to talk only about *land value.*

So the question is *this*: Is the present "true value" on this land suitable? We don't think it is. And we don't believe you will either when you look at some of the facts with us.

Whenever I have come here in the past asking for a change, I have never asked for favors or for any preferential treatment— and we are not asking for favors or preferential treatment today. I am not the owner, and I am not on a percentage basis. Neither is the appraiser. We have made a diligent, impartial effort to find out what the "true value" on this land *should* be. *That* is what we are asking you for, and that is *all* we are asking you for.

I really don't need to tell you about this appraiser. He was retained because he is widely recognized as an expert in such matters. I think you are going to be fascinated by some of the things he has to show you.

APPRAISER.   (*Rising*) First, let's take a quick look at this parcel. (*Uncovers drawing on easel*)

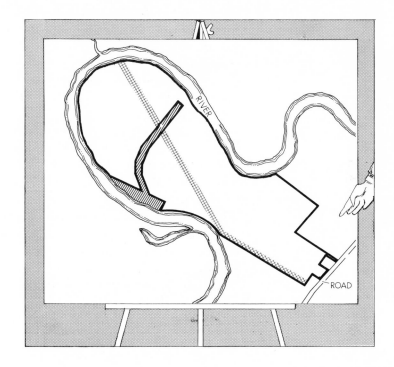

This heavy line bounds the Willow Creek land that we are concerned with here this morning. The developers of Willow Creek began buying this land on contract from Mrs. Johnson in 1972. The price was only about $1,000 per acre. This purchase did not include Mrs. Johnson's house or the home-site.

In 1973, the developer bought a narrow strip of land—shown here by the stripes—from the City. The price: $1,000 per acre.

Why were the per-acre prices so low in these two arm's-length sales? If you look at the subject land carefully, there's really no big mystery.

1. The awkward shape is, of course, obvious.

2. The only access to this tract is via Stone Road—and this sizable tract has less than 250 feet of frontage along Stone Road. Very skimpy indeed.

3. Further, over one-third of this land is in flood plain, and water stands on consider-able portions year round.

4. Still further, a power-transmission-line easement—shown here in the cross-hatching—runs across the south side, along here, and then off in a northwest-erly direction. That's where the develop-ers decided to put the entry drive, partly flanking the transmission towers.

It is not surprising, is it, that other develop-ers had passed over this site? It has been made into an attractive golf course, but its alternative uses were clearly limited. That is why this tract brought only a little over $1,000 per acre.

Next, let's see how Willow Creek compares

with the other golf courses in this area. Here (*uncovering chart*) . . .

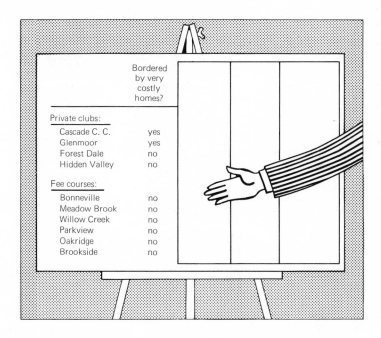

	Bordered by very costly homes?
Private clubs:	
Cascade C. C.	yes
Glenmoor	yes
Forest Dale	no
Hidden Valley	no
Fee courses:	
Bonneville	no
Meadow Brook	no
Willow Creek	no
Parkview	no
Oakridge	no
Brookside	no

. . . is a summary of all of the full-length courses in High City which are privately owned.

(*Noticing board members starting to take notes from the chart*) It isn't necessary to write any of this down. If you like, I'll furnish you with enough copies of these summaries so each board member can have a set.

The first four golf courses listed here are private country clubs; only members and their invited guests may play. The other six—including Willow Creek—are fee courses; they are open to anyone.

Two of the private country clubs—Cascade and Glenmoor—are bordered by very prestigious homes. None of the others are. Oh, there are some pleasant homes backing up to Willow Creek—backing up to the power transmission line—but they couldn't be called, by any stretch, very prestigious homes.

On this chart, these ten golf courses were not just listed in random order. They were ranked by the size of their greens fees. (*Removes cover over one column.*)

	Bordered by very costly homes?	Greens fees	
Private clubs:			
Cascade C. C.	yes	$12.00	
Glenmoor	yes	7.00	
Forest Dale	no	7.00	
Hidden Valley	no	6.00	
Fee courses:			
Bonneville	no	$ 5.00	
Meadow Brook	no	4.50	
Willow Creek	no	4.50	
Parkview	no	4.50	
Oakridge	no	4.25	
Brookside	no	3.25	

And, as it happens, this is a pretty fair ranking of these courses in order of prestige. Oh, one might want to change the order a bit—my own judgment is that Hidden Valley is a better course than Forest Dale—but, by and large, this is a *generally* fair ranking, itn't it?

Golf courses—especially fee courses—are often built on land that is not too attractive for other uses. One of the limiting factors is flood plain. As you can see (*removing cover from another column*), . . .

	Bordered by very costly homes?	Greens fees	Over 1/3 in flood plain?
Private clubs:			
Cascade C. C.	yes	$12.00	no
Glenmoor	yes	7.00	no
Forest Dale	no	7.00	no
Hidden Valley	no	6.00	no
Fee courses:			
Bonneville	no	$ 5.00	yes
Meadow Brook	no	4.50	no
Willow Creek	no	4.50	yes
Parkview	no	4.50	yes
Oakridge	no	4.25	no
Brookside	no	3.25	yes

. . . four of the fee courses have one-third or more of their areas in flood plain. Willow Creek is one of them. None of the private country clubs is so afflicted. I might mention that I retained a graduate planner to work up this flood plain information for me, and he did not know which of the golf courses was under study. Meadow Brook is not as burdened with flood plain, but it has its own limitations: bordering railroad tracks and flight easements over most of its land area.

Keep in mind that most of these golf courses have quite long frontages along public streets and roads, while Willow Creek has very little frontage. For alternative (non-golf course) uses, some of these other tracts could be sold off for several times what the subject land would bring.

How do the "true values" on these ten golf courses compare? It would be reasonable to expect the per-acre land values to be ranked in roughly the same order as the golf courses are ranked on this chart, wouldn't it? Well *(removing cover from the last column),* . . .

	Bordered by very costly homes?	Greens fees	Over 1/3 in flood plain?	Assessor's "true value" per acre of golf course
Private clubs:				
Cascade C. C.	yes	$12.00	no	$3,400
Glenmoor	yes	7.00	no	3,500
Forest Dale	no	7.00	no	2,200
Hidden Valley	no	6.00	no	2,800
Fee courses:				
Bonneville	no	$ 5.00	yes	$1,200
Meadow Brook	no	4.50	no	1,200
Willow Creek	no	4.50	yes	1,200
Parkview	no	4.50	yes	1,170
Oakridge	no	4.25	no	1,200
Brookside	no	3.25	yes	1,200

they *are.* It is gratifying to see how well they
do fall in line. The assessment officials who

had something to do with this should be commended.

Now, since the $1,200-per-acre value for the subject land is so obviously in line, what are we doing here this morning?

	Bordered by very costly homes?	Greens fees	Over 1/3 in flood plain?	Assessor's "true value" per acre of golf course
Private clubs:				
Cascade C. C.	yes	$12.00	no	$3,400
Glenmoor	yes	7.00	no	3,500
Forest Dale	no	7.00	no	2,200
Hidden Valley	no	6.00	no	2,800
Fee courses:				
Bonneville	no	$ 5.00	yes	$1,200
Meadow Brook	no	4.50	no	1,200
Willow Creek	no	4.50	yes	1,200
Parkview	no	4.50	yes	1,170
Oakridge	no	4.25	no	1,200
Brookside	no	3.25	yes	1,200

Well, the answer is that the assessment on the Willow Creek land is *not* $1,200 per acre. (*Removes flap.*)
It's *$3,500 per acre.*

	Bordered by very costly homes?	Greens fees	Over 1/3 in flood plain?	Assessor's "true value" per acre of golf course
Private clubs:				
Cascade C. C.	yes	$12.00	no	$3,400
Glenmoor	yes	7.00	no	3,500
Forest Dale	no	7.00	no	2,200
Hidden Valley	no	6.00	no	2,800
Fee courses:				
Bonneville	no	$ 5.00	yes	$1,200
Meadow Brook	no	4.50	no	1,200
Willow Creek	no	4.50	yes	**3,500**
Parkview	no	4.50	yes	1,170
Oakridge	no	4.25	no	1,200
Brookside	no	3.25	yes	1,200

Just *one number* on this chart . . . stands out like the proverbial sore thumb. *That* is why we are here this morning.

Willow Creek is not the only one of these golf courses that was ever overassessed. In the 1969 reassessment, three of the other fee courses were given "true values" like Willow Creek's. All three were appealed. Here is what happened. (*Uncovers chart.*)

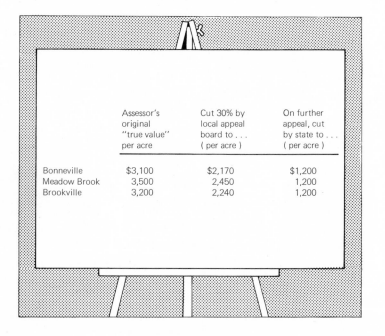

	Assessor's original "true value" per acre	Cut 30% by local appeal board to . . . (per acre)	On further appeal, cut by state to . . . (per acre)
Bonneville	$3,100	$2,170	$1,200
Meadow Brook	3,500	2,450	1,200
Brookville	3,200	2,240	1,200

The County Board of Review cut each by 30 percent. Then, on further appeal, the State Tax Board reduced each to $1,200 per acre.

Can you look at these figures and doubt what the state would decide in this case? There doesn't seem to be much doubt in this case about what *will* be done. The only question seems to be *by whom*; will this board face up to what clearly should be done or will this board pass the buck to the state, knowing that it will do the right thing?

A final point. In studying this case, I worked up a lot of data—data on zoning, utility lines, yardages, sprinklers, and other factors—which I haven't even mentioned. I have confined this to the most salient points because I respect your time. However, (*turning to assessor and speaking softly*) I do not want to walk out of here and have someone say, "Yes, but what he *didn't* tell you was *this*." If there is a telling point that I haven't covered, will you please raise it now.

BOARD MEMBER.	You mentioned sprinklers. Can you tell us which of these courses have sprinkler systems installed?
APPRAISER.	All have watered fairways except Parkview and Brookside.
ASSESSOR.	You seem to make a *great deal* out of the fact that this golf course has so little frontage and has water on it. Well, I'm not a golfer, but I know people who do play, and they told me that they like to have quiet when they're playing. The frontage is certainly big enough for golfers to get in and out, isn't it? A lot of cars going past along the golf course wouldn't help the players, and it could even be a nuisance. And some people think water on a golf course is nice, don't they?
APPRAISER.	It seems to me that there is a perfectly logical and satisfying answer to your questions.

Willow Creek *does* have enough frontage for adequate ingress and egress—*for a golf course*. And the water, standing there *is* attractive . . . *on a golf course*.

However, if you are going to try to support a "true value" of much over $1,200 per acre for the basic land—and remember that golf course site improvements are not normally assessed in this state—you must have some potential *alternative* use in mind. And for most alternative uses, some of these things—skimpy frontage, awkward shape, flood plain, and power-transmission easement—would be quite limiting, wouldn't they?

ATTORNEY. Look at it this way. Parts of the Cascade Country Club land could be sold off for several thousands of dollars per acre—several times what the Willow Creek land is worth. The same thing could be said about some of the other courses.

BOARD MEMBER. I think what he (*inclining her head to indicate the appraiser, but addressing herself to the assessor*) is saying is that $1,200 per acre is fine if this is golf course land, but $3,500 is too high. If we're going to say this land is worth $3,500 per acre, then we have to be able to say what else the land is good for that would justify it.

APPRAISER. (*Smiling and nodding approvingly at board member*) Yes, that is *exactly* what "he" is trying to say. (*Sits*)

BOARD CHAIRPERSON. (*Looking around table*) Is there anything else?

ATTORNEY. I would just like to add this. We made an honest effort to come up with the right, the fair recommendation. We were not swayed by the client. We did not say, "Suppose we ask for this, and then maybe they'll settle for that." I think we have made a clear showing that the "true value" should be $1,200 per acre—and we will pursue this matter until it *is* $1,200 per acre.

BOARD CHAIRPERSON. (*To appraiser*) I believe you said that you would be willing to furnish us with copies of what you have on the large charts. We would like to have them.

BOARD MEMBER. And you might include any other information on golf courses that you think we might be interested in, for this or other cases.

BOARD CHAIRPERSON. Thank you all very much.

Epilog: Some weeks later, the review board met to make its decision. One member moved that the "true value" be dropped to $1,200 per acre. Another seconded. The vote was unanimous.

Chapter 13

Other Ways to Get Your Taxes Reduced

Anyone may so arrange his affairs that his taxes shall be as low as possible; he is not bound to choose that pattern which will best pay the Treasury; there is not even a patriotic duty to increase one's taxes.

—Judge Learned Hand

How can you arrange your affairs so that *your* property taxes are as low as possible? Making sure that your assessed value is fair is, of course, very important. But there is much more that you should consider.

CAN YOU SAVE EVEN IF YOU DON'T OWN ANY REAL ESTATE?

On the theory that part of the typical rental payment is imputable to real estate taxes, a growing number of states have provided for tax relief for certain *renters*—particularly low-income and elderly persons. Find out if your state has joined this group and if you are eligible.

APPLY FOR EXEMPTIONS OR PROPERTY TAX RELIEF AND SAVE?

Property taxes can work hardships on some people (elderly, farmers, and others, who are often members of politically potent groups), so states have provided many forms of property tax relief.

Elderly and Low-Income Persons

All of the states now have programs to reduce the property taxes of at least some of their senior citizens, particularly those with low incomes. These programs are usually of one of these two types: the so-called circuit-breaker approach (a credit or rebate is given when property taxes exceed a specified percentage of the taxpayer's income) or taxation only above a certain level.

Incredibly, about a million people who are eligible for savings under circuit breakers alone have not taken advantage of them, according to an authoritative 1975 estimate.

Owners of Farmland and Open Space Land

By late 1973, 31 states had laws to treat certain lands differently. Primarily, the thrust was to value farmland on the basis of its actual use rather than on its potential highest and best use, so that farmers could afford to continue farming their lands despite rapidly rising land values in many areas. In some states, this differential treatment can apply to certain forest, open space, and recreational tracts as well.

Others

In some states, exemptions or relief are extended to many others including homeowners, veterans, surviving dependents of veterans, disabled persons, those with mortgage loans, and others.

Legislation for all 50 states and the District of Columbia are summarized in the Supplements. However, these summaries cannot be complete, and the laws and practices are subject to change over time. So, to make sure you know about all the opportunities in your state, telephone or write your state property tax agency, local tax authority, and/or your attorney and accountant.

NOTIFY THE ASSESSOR OF CHANGES IN YOUR PROPERTY AND SAVE?

After your property has been assessed, important changes may take place which will entitle you to a reduction.

What kind of changes? Reduction in land size because a public or quasipublic agency acquires part or because public rights-of-way are dedicated. Reduction in the value of the improvements because of damage or destruction by fire, vandalism, termites, or other means. Reduction in property value because of substantial changes in location and use factors.

Sometimes, people continue to pay taxes for years on improvements that were destroyed, or on portions of land they no longer own. Do not just assume that the assessor knows about such important changes. *Make sure.*

USE YOUR ASSESSMENT TO SAVE ON INCOME TAXES?

The *total amount* of your assessment may not be all that counts. The *allocation* of the assessed value *between land and improvements* can be important too.

Say you have just paid $100,000 for a parcel with a four-apartment building on it. The land is not depreciable for income tax purposes, but the improvements are. How much of the $100,000 can you allocate to the depreciable improvements? The general rule is that the allocation should be *in proportion* to the relative market values of the land and improvements. The allocation might be based on an appraisal or on recent sales in the area. But an often-used basis is the ratio of land and improvement figures in the tax assessment on the property in question. Since this alternative can be checked quickly and at no cost and since assessors often assign a disproportionately high percentage of the assessed value to improvements, reasons for the popularity of this basis are rather obvious.

CHANGE THE WAY YOU TREAT REAL ESTATE TAXES WHEN FIGURING YOUR INCOME TAXES AND SAVE?

When it's time to figure income taxes, there are some alternatives that are not well known but can be helpful.

Example: It is sometimes possible (and sometimes advantageous) to deduct real estate taxes in one year even though they are not actually paid until the next year.

Example: If you own unimproved and unproductive real property, you may be able to choose each year between (1) treating the real estate taxes as an expense or (2) capitalizing the real estate taxes (adding them to your cost basis or other basis on which you figure depreciation), depending upon which is more advantageous to you in that particular year.

USE A TAX-STOP CLAUSE IN YOUR LEASE AND SAVE?

Thousands of landlords are protected against possible future increases in real estate taxes by lease clauses which require the tenants to pay part or all of such increases. The most common form cites an amount of annual real estate tax as the *base amount* (usually either as an actual dollar amount or as the amount payable in a specified year) and then provides that the tenant will reimburse the landlord for all or a specified part of any real estate taxes in excess of the base amount during the term of the lease. If there is more than one tenant in a property, each may be required to make reimbursement on a pro rata basis.

LOOK OUT FOR ABUSES OF TAX-STOP CLAUSES AND SAVE?

The real estate tax burdens on major income properties are usually both a bit complicated in computation and substantial in amount. So, if there is an agreement to share the tax burden, both opportunities and temptations to abuse the situation can arise.

Because leases are often signed before construction is complete (and therefore before the final assessment is known), the base amount in the tax clause is often defined as the amount of the tax bill for the first full year which reflects the complete assessment on the completed property. In an area where tax rates are marching upward, the developer-lessor of an office building or shopping center or whatever may be sorely tempted to tell the assessor that construction is, for all practical purposes, 100 percent complete despite the fact there are uncompleted areas.

Once the base amount is determined, a landlord who is to be reimbursed for most or all of any increases in the real estate taxes may see little or no incentive to challenge subsequent increases in the assessment, even if they appear quite unreasonable; thus, the tenants may be exposed to the ineptitude or caprice of the assessor.

It is not unusual for tenants to retain property tax specialists to see that they are not bearing more of a tax burden than they should.

REWRITE (OR RECHECK) YOUR
LEGAL DESCRIPTION AND SAVE?

A natural tendency for those (lawyers, surveyors, and others) who make up legal descriptions is to make the descriptions as all-inclusive as possible. This normally stems from a (laudable) desire to make sure that no interests meant to be included are omitted from the description.

These legal descriptions appear in deeds and other instruments which are made a part of public records—and come to the attention of assessors and of those who make up tax maps for assessors. Very often, the land size set out in the first deed that identifies any particular parcel is recorded on the assessor's property description card.

Now, you can see the point we are coming to, but let's put it into sharp focus with this simple example:

> Say a corner parcel has a gross area of (200 × 200 feet) 40,000 square feet. Each of the two bordering public streets has a permanent 30-foot-wide right-of-way over this parcel.

> One can describe this site as having an area of 40,000 square feet, more or less, subject to existing public street rights-of-way—in which case there's good chance the parcel will be assessed for 40,000 square feet in many districts.

> Or one can describe the same tract by citing the same (gross) dimensions, part being subject to public street rights-of-way and the balance having a net area of 28,900 square feet, more or less—in which case you may end up with a much smaller assessment.

This is such an obvious example that we would like to believe that no assessor would work in such a hit-or-miss fashion. However, the fact is that many do.

And many land-area problems are more complex. Estimating the area of a very irregular parcel (some have more than 25 different courses) can be difficult. Surveyors sometimes find "surplus" land which may or may not be legally a part of the particular parcel they are working on. Actual dimensions often vary from dimensions set out in deeds and plats.

Sometimes, saving money is as simple as (1) thinking about property tax consequences when one writes a new legal description or (2) filing an affidavit and/or corrective deed to make an old legal description more accurate.

MERGE TWO OR MORE PARCELS AND SAVE?

In areas where some of the farms are being divided into homesites, small sites often sell for several times as much *per acre* as larger sites. A 1-acre site may sell for $3,000 while a nearby 15-acre site sells for $750 per acre—only one-quarter as much per acre.

Some assessors have adopted guidelines to recognize this general effect. In their districts, there may be an opportunity to save any time there are separately assessed adjacent parcels with related (but not identical) ownerships. Even many real estate professionals are unaware of it, but uniting two 20-acre tracts can lower real estate taxes 25 percent or more. Uniting three 1-acre parcels can reduce the tax burden by as much as 40 percent.

CHOOSE A DIFFERENT LOCALE AND SAVE?

It is no secret that property tax burdens are hideously uneven from place to place. *Where* you choose a site can make a big difference.

Governor Wendell R. Anderson of Minnesota gave this example: "There was an example that I am fond of citing, a particular farmer who has part of his farm in our State, part in our neighboring State. On that part of his farm in our State, real estate taxes went down 19 percent. That part of his farm that lies in an adjacent State went up 29 percent."

According to federal figures, state and local property taxes per capita in 1972–73 were over twice as high in the state of New York as in adjacent Pennsylvania.

And inducements to attract prospective employers into an area can be substantial. For example, Louisiana has an exemption for certain industrial properties for a period of ten years.

However, it is not necessary to move from state to state to make important savings. Sometimes, one need only choose a property in another neighborhood . . . or just across the street.

TIME YOUR NEW CONSTRUCTION TO SAVE?

Generally, taxable properties are taxed as of a certain date each year; improvements added after that date are not taxed until the following year. So, timing of new construction can make an important difference.

In cases involving new construction, it can be useful to have some convincing record of the stage of completion on this effective date. In active districts, it is not possible for assessors to go out on the effective date and judge the state of completion of all improvements under construction on that one day. Sometimes it is months before the assessor inquires into the state of completion on the effective date. And even if the assessor does make a timely inspection, you have no assurance that the stage of completion will be judged accurately. In some cases, a brief letter report by the builder as of the effective date and dated photos may suffice. On large projects, taking the trouble to get an inspection report by an expert appraiser, architect, and/or contractor may be very wise.

CHANGE YOUR DESIGN AND SAVE?—I

Modifying the design of a structure in order to save on real estate taxes is not a new idea. The story goes that both the mansard roof (which is not a roof at all but a particular treatment of the top floor) and French doors (which look so much like windows) were created in response to tax assessing by the number of floors and by the number of doors.

Well, tax assessing may be a little more sophisticated today, but considering the real estate tax consequences of various design alternatives can still be important. This is particularly true with certain types of income properties for which property taxes are the largest single item of operating expense.

It is common for developers of buildings to weigh the additional costs of sprinkler systems against the savings in insurance premiums that would result. Too often overlooked in this decision is the likely increase in the real estate tax burden because of the sprinklers. Similarly, likely real estate tax consequences can be factored into important design decisions including higher-initial-cost versus reduced-maintenance-costs and higher-initial-cost versus lower-utility-cost decisions.

CHANGE YOUR DESIGN AND SAVE?—II

In addition, there are special tax breaks deliberately set up to influence design. For example, an Indiana law provides for an annual deduction of up to $2,000 from the assessed valuation on any real property which is equipped with a solar energy heating or cooling system. New Hampshire has also authorized localities to grant tax exemptions on homes equipped with solar heating or cooling devices.

FIX UP YOUR PROPERTY WITHOUT AN INCREASE IN YOUR ASSESSMENT?

Improvements to an existing building which do not increase its size substantially are often ignored by assessors.

This is what Arthur D. Little, Inc., found in a study of property taxes in the major United States cities:

> . . . most improvements do not, in fact, result in reassessment. . . . Obviously, local assessors do not want to discourage private reconstruction efforts. In fact, in most central cities in our sample even improvements to commercial properties were seldom reassessed, although the frequency was higher than for residential properties. In most cities tremendous confusion reigns as to reassessment policy. Again and again, investors reported that they thought they would be reassessed for improvements which, according to the Assessor's Office, never lead to reassessment.

To help dispel such confusion, some cities actually publish information on improvements that will *not* result in reassessments. For example, information from a pamphlet published by San Francisco's assessor is set out on the next page.

FIX UP YOUR PROPERTY AND SAVE?

In certain locales, it is even possible to get your real estate tax burden *reduced* as a result of making improvements. For example, to encourage landlords to bring their properties up to housing code standards, Boston embarked on a two-year experimental program enabling a resident landlord of a one-to-three-unit dwelling to qualify to deduct from his real estate tax bill 10 percent of the costs of repairs and improvements.

SAVE ON AN APPEAL EVEN IF
THE ASSESSMENT ISN'T REDUCED?

It may be a little hard to believe at first, but it is technically possible to appeal an assessment, fail to get it reduced, and still save money.

Consider this hypothetical example. Mr. A builds a major shopping mall in Indianapolis. It takes A three years to complete the center. Each spring, the assessor increases the assessment to reflect the state of completion. Each time A receives a notice from the assessor, he appeals. Each time taxes are due, A pays an amount *he* thinks is fair, an amount much less than he is billed. A argues before the county board of review, then before the state tax board. From first appeal to final determination, this appeal process takes over three years. Finally, the state tax board decides that the original assessments will stand—unchanged. A decides to accept the decision, not to appeal to a court. Now A has to pay in the rest of the real estate taxes (that he would have paid anyway) *plus interest*. But A has saved a lot of money. How? Well, in A's state, the interest is computed at a true rate of 6 percent, and there is no penalty. In effect, A has had the use of this money for 6 percent during a period when he would have paid 9 or 10 percent to borrow the same money.

OFFICIAL LIST OF HOME IMPROVEMENTS WHICH WILL NOT INCREASE YOUR ASSESSMENT [SAN FRANCISCO]

Inside the Home

New furnace (not necessarily same type)
Automatic hot water heater
Plaster repairs
Redecorating (painting, wallpaper)
Added small closets or minor built-ins
New ceilings
Interior surfacing
Repair, replace wiring (incl. 220-volt)
Replace plumbing and light fixtures
New floor surfacing
Leveling a floor
Lateral loads (adding stiffness for earthquake loads)
Addition of vents to unvented heaters
Remodel fireplace
New fire exit (inside house)
Replace cabinets and counter tops
Ventilating fan in bathroom
New sink and garbage disposal
Foundation repairs and ratproofing

Outside the Home

Repointing, repairing, and replacing exterior masonry
New roof
Repairing and replacing porches, steps, and stairs
Remove unused porch or exterior trim
Repair to fire escapes
New fire escapes
Replacing window sashes and sills
Insulation, weatherstripping, storm windows and doors
Exterior awnings and window shutters
Add or replace gutter, downspouts
Outside painting, asbestos siding
Minor repair of dry rot and termite damage
Repair, replace garage doors
Decorative screens, minor sculptures, etc.
Homeowner connection to new underground wiring
Street trees
Repair, replace sidewalks

Garage and Grounds

Outdoor electric cable and outdoor lights
Repairing or replacing private walks
Replacing dilapidated sheds and garages (same type, same area)
Paving rear lot parking area
New fences or walls
Addition of retaining walls
Lawns, landscaping, lawn sprinklers (joint backyards)
New sheds to store garbage and rubbish containers

Note: It should be emphasized that a *combination* of these improvements could result in a considerable increase in market value of your property. If this happens, state law requires that adjustment of assessed values be reflected in proportion to the increase in market value.

73

If you are weighing the pros and cons of appealing the assessment on a major income property (or already have an appeal under way), perhaps you will want to recheck certain provisions of the law in *your* state.

BUY A PROPERTY WITH AN OVERASSESSMENT AND SAVE?

In a way, a property with a terrible overassessment may represent an opportunity.

A property burdened with an unreasonable assessment may be sold for much less than it would have brought if it had had a fair assessment. Many who buy such properties promptly appeal the assessments, citing as part of their grounds for reduction the price just paid in the open market.

USE AN ASSESSMENT IN A CONDEMNATION TRIAL AND WIN?

In certain circumstances, a much-too-high assessment can be used to the property owner's *advantage*.

Suppose a public agency is acquiring a home in an urban renewal area. The owner doesn't think the agency's offer of $12,000 is high enough, and a jury trial is held to determine just compensation. Experts testify that the property is worth from $11,000 to $13,000. However, this piece of evidence is offered: The owner has been paying taxes for years which are based on an assessor's valuation of $19,700. Even if the jurors decide the assessor probably didn't know what he was doing, they may feel sympathy for the owner and resentment for government agencies. ("Sure, a lousy appraisal like that is all right for a guy to pay taxes on for years, but when the time comes to take his property, then they find a *qualified* appraiser. Well, it's not right!")

And trial verdicts often reflect such subjective feelings.

LOBBY FOR CHANGES MORE
EFFECTIVELY AND SAVE?

Do you feel that one class of property is treated unfairly in your state? Is there some assessment procedure you would particularly like to see changed?

If so, you are not limited merely to the appeal procedures. Far from it. Some of the alternative approaches:

1. Retain a property tax expert to prepare a brief on the particular subject, which could be given to the state property tax authority for consideration. (Alternatively, it could be given to the press, state legislators, the governor, review board members, and/or others.)

2. Join and work with a citizens' group seeking property tax reform. Reportedly, every state has one or more, and the Tax Reform Research Group of Washington, D.C., has attempted to act as a clearinghouse for some of their campaigns.

3. If you are challenging an increase in the assessment on an apartment project or shopping center you own or manage and you have a newsletter, keep your tenants informed with simple, honest articles about this upward pressure on rents. And send a copy of each newsletter to the assessor or the review board.

4. Periodically, tax officials in some states and locales name ad hoc citizen committees to advise them on changes that should be made. If that's what happens in your area, find out who is on the committee dealing with your particular area of interest, and tell them of your feelings.

These few examples plus a little ingenuity may suggest some other alternatives to you.

SUPPLEMENTS

Supplements A, B, and C show additional methods for checking the fairness of an assessed value and for estimating what an assessed value *should* be.

The last eleven supplements (D through N) are summaries of legislation and practice in the 50 states and the District of Columbia. These have been abstracted from numerous federal publications.

Principal sources include:

Advisory Commission on Intergovernmental Relations

Commerce Clearing House

Subcommittee on Intergovernmental Relations to the Committee on Government Operations of the United States Senate

U.S. Department of Agriculture

U.S. Department of Commerce

Summarizing legislation and practice in so many states is difficult, and the various laws and practices are subject to change. The author assumes no responsibility for errors or omissions which may have occurred. Taxpayers who want to know how the law in a particular state applies to a particular property are urged to consult state or local tax officials and qualified professionals.

USING THE THREE
APPROACHES TO VALUE

How to Check the Assessor's Cost Approach

> . . . the assessor usually bases his determination of the fair market value of a given property on an estimate of its depreciated reproduction cost. The estimates are drawn from detailed tables and formulas which purportedly represent the determinants of the market value of similar properties, and therefore can be used in place of objective data on the market value of the property under consideration . . .
>
> Assessments based upon estimates of depreciated reproduction cost however, involve consideration of only a few of the determinants of the market value of the real property . . .
>
> *—Stephen F. LeRoy in the Federal Reserve Bank of Kansas City's Monthly Review*

In valuing buildings and other improvements, most assessors set out only one approach in any detail: the cost approach. So, if you are going to review the assessor's work on an improved property, you normally want to find the answer to these questions:

Is the assessor's estimate of reproduction cost higher than the actual construction cost? If so, you can show that it is in a simple, straightforward way:

	Actual cost	Assessor's estimate of reproduction cost
Building	$215,350	$257,390
Carports	14,227	16,740
Paving	2,850	2,100
Fencing	740	600
Improvements	$233,167	$276,830
Land	30,000	37,500
Total	$263,167	$314,330

(These cost figures include allowance for contractor's profit and indirect costs.)

Remember that the contractor's profit and indirect costs are a normal part of building costs. Omitting them in an appeal on behalf of a builder-owner may unfairly understate the actual costs of a project.

In figuring reproduction costs, did the assessor follow the manual properly? Typically, an assessor is required to use a real property appraisal manual issued by a state agency. For a variety of reasons, assessors often fail to select the proper cost factors from these manuals.

To answer this question, a parcel owner may or may not need the help of an expert, depending upon the nature of the improvements and upon the owner's expertise.

Are cost factors set out in the manual too high? The cost figures set out in the state manuals are usually *below* typical costs, but not always. The test is whether they are out of line with typical construction costs and with authoritative cost manuals.

Is the assessor's estimate of reproduction cost for your property out of line with those on similar properties? If so, the discrepancy should be fairly obvious in a side by side comparison like this:

Apartment project	Quality of construction	Assessor's quality-of-construction rating		Assessor's est. of reproduction cost per sq ft of bldg.
Subject Property	Par	B + 5	(Ave. + 28%)	$18.55
Colonial Square	Very similar	C	(Average)	$14.35
Williamsburg Apts.	A little better than subject	C + 5	(Ave. + 5%)	$15.15
Woodcrest Villas	A little poorer	C − 5	(Ave. − 5%)	$13.65
Brookwood Manor	Very similar	C	(Average)	$14.90
Forest Hills Apts.	Very similar	C	(Average)	$14.35
Kensington Apts.	Very similar	C	(Average)	$14.15

Did the assessor include any improvements which are not usually assessed? Did the assessor value improvements on your property—let's say landscaping for example—usually excluded in valuing other properties of the same type?

Did the assessor estimate the status of construction accurately? If construction was not complete on the effective tax date, see if the assessor's estimated percentage of completion is fair.

Did the assessor make proper use of the depreciation guidelines set out in the manual? Most real property appraisal manuals issued by the states include tables which purport to give average depreciation percentages for buildings of various ages and conditions. These tables may look impressive, but they are not reliable appraisal tools.

In using these tables, the choice of a depreciation percentage is left largely to the *judgment* of the assessor. For a given effective building age, the assessor's *unsupported opinion* of condition and attractiveness alone can make a difference of 40 percent in this "value estimate." And we have already seen some indications of just how appallingly undeveloped and carelessly exercised that judgment is in many cases. Often, these depreciation tables are merely the justification (*cover* might be a better choice of words) for whatever depreciation percentages assessors want to use.

Even so, if the assessor set out an estimated age and a rating of condition and attractiveness for your building, take a moment to see if they are consistent with the depreciation percentage supposedly selected from the manual.

Did the assessor allow for "unusual" depreciation? If all buildings lost value at the same steady rate, then estimating depreciation would be a simple matter of saying something like this: "This building is 26 years old, so its accrued depreciation is 47.5 percent." But a building does not lose value at a steady rate over the years. And the rate of depreciation for one building can be much different from that of a look-alike building in a different location. It is even possible for a brand new building to have a higher percentage of accrued depreciation than a 30-year-old building.

So even if your assessor's table *did* reflect *average* depreciation for a structure like yours of a given age and condition (and there is probably little or no objective proof that it *does*), is that a fair estimate of depreciation for *your particular building?* It might be fair. It might be terribly wrong. The simple fact is that a depreciation table like your assessor uses cannot give you the answer.

Therefore, it is often necessary to borrow tools from the other two approaches to gauge depreciation reliably. Here are two quick examples:

> In a condominium development, the assessor may insist on higher values for certain units—say those built on a prototype plan called the Tree House—because they cost more to build. However, if sales clearly show that these more-cost-to-build Tree House units typically sell for less than the others because their design is not as popular with buyers, you may have a good argument for

a reduction in assessment because of functional obsolescence—a form of depreciation best reflected in this case by the market data approach.

Say a three-year-old shopping center never attained over 50 percent occupancy because of overbuilding in its submarket. There is a strong basis for a large reduction for economic obsolescence, a form of depreciation usually best demonstrated in such cases by the income approach.

The Darling of the "Dry Labbers." Expertly used, the cost approach can be very helpful in some cases. In a relatively few assessment jurisdictions, the cost approach *is* expertly used. In far more, its use is but a crude aping of sound appraising.

In chemistry courses, some crafty students just *guess* how experiments are supposed to work out instead of performing the assigned laboratory work. Then they fake a report on "what they found." This is sometimes called "dry labbing" because these students don't even get their test tubes wet. Well, there's a lot of dry labbing in the assessment field too. And the unsupported, unrefined cost approach is the darling of the dry labbers.

Supplement B

How to Use the Market Data Approach

For several decades it was popular in assessors' circles to pontificate on the difference between prices and values. Prices were what gullible persons paid for properties; values were what assessors in their omniscience decided the properties were worth. There are still some assessors who subscribe to such nonsense, but most of the assessors I know concede that sales prices, with all their imperfections, are the best evidence of value in most instances.

—Ronald B. Welch, Assistant Executive Secretary, Property Taxes, California State Board of Equalization

In most cases, the assessor's most crucial task is to estimate market value. So, in most cases, the basic question should be something like this: How many dollars would this property bring if it were offered and sold under certain circumstances?

And in most cases, the best way to answer this question is to use the market data approach to value.

COMPARISONS OF WHOLE PROPERTIES

Let's say it is *your* job to estimate the current market value of an attractive single-family dwelling at 330 North Fairfield Street. In effect, you are to estimate what price this dwelling would bring if it were offered and sold on a typical arm's-length basis.

Because you want to do a good job, you will give appropriate consideration to all three approaches to value, but the market data approach is likely to be your best approach *if similar properties in the same market area are frequently offered and sold.* You choose several representative sales which are most similar to the subject parcel at 330 North Fairfield. You begin with the prices that these properties sold for, adjust these prices for any changes in this market since the sales were made and for individual property differences, and you have some good indications of what price the subject property would probably bring. An example of this procedure is set out on the next page.

85

SUMMARY OF MARKET DATA APPROACH TO VALUE

Selection of Comparables: These twelve comparables were selected as particularly good indicators of the value of the subject dwelling. Each is located either in the same neighborhood or a very similar neighborhood. Each was sold earlier this year on an arm's-length basis, and no adjustments were considered necessary for either the time or the conditions of sale. Each comparable dwelling, like the subject dwelling, is a 2-story and basement, frame, 3-bedroom dwelling.

Address of comparable	Sale price	Comments on comparison with subject	Value indication for subject property
1019 Riverton	$47,500	On balance, judged equivalent	$47,500
1224 Riverton	55,000	Less $7,000 to reflect comparable's extra lot	48,000
1300 Redwood Dr.	46,500	On balance, judged equivalent	46,500
216 Canyon Dr.	47,800	On balance, judged equivalent	47,800
237 Canyon Dr.	51,000	Less $3,500 to reflect contributing value of comparable's pool, deck, better plantings	47,500
405 Canyon Dr.	47,000	On balance, judged equivalent	47,000
773 Canyon Dr.	45,000	Plus $2,000 to reflect subject's larger living area	47,000
415 N. Fairfield	47,500	Very similar	47,500
427 N. Fairfield	50,000	Less $2,500 to reflect comparable's finished basement with fireplace	47,500
780 Willow Creek Dr.	49,200	Less $1,500 for comparable's additional lavatory, intercom, and central vacuum	47,700

Address of comparable	Sale price	Comments on comparison with subject	Value indication for subject property
786 Willow Creek Dr.	48,000	On balance, judged equivalent	48,000
1006 Willow Creek Dr.	45,000	Plus $2,000 for subject's larger lot and better plantings	47,000
Estimate of market value:		These indications of the value of the subject property were quite consistent, so consistent that no serious effort at correlation was needed.	$47,500
Conversion to fair assessed value:		If the required (legal) assessment ratio in your area is $1/2$ but similar properties are typically assessed at $1/5$ of market value (the de facto level), then a fair assessment on your property should be on the order of ($1/5$ of $47,500).	$ 9,500

UNITS OF COMPARISON

Normally, dwellings are compared with one another on a whole-property basis. However, other types of property are often compared with one another on the basis of meaningful *units* of comparison. Some examples:

Type of property	Common units of comparison (value per . . .)
Residential lots, commercial sites	Front foot, square foot
Suburban tracts, farms, large industrial tracts	Acre
Apartments	Apartment, rentable room, square foot of gross building area, square foot of net building area
Office buildings	Square foot of gross building area, square foot of net rentable area
Motels	Rental room
Motor freight terminals	Dock door

Using meaningful units of comparison, one can often make intelligent comparisons between two properties which have several important similarities but are of different sizes.

GROSS RENT MULTIPLIERS

Let's say an income property rents for $10,000 per year and that it has just sold for $60,000. That sale reflected a gross annual rent multiplier of 6.

Further, let's say five other recent sales reflected gross rent multipliers ranging from 5½ to 6½, and that all six of these comparables are quite similar to an income property we are appraising. Now, if we know that our subject property rents for, say, $12,000 per year, we already have a fair idea of its market value (5½ to 6½ × $12,000 = $66,000 to $78,000), don't we?

Income properties are often compared on the basis of gross rent multipliers, as in the example on the next page.

This is a useful method which is sometimes employed by assessors, but be on the outlook for two common abuses of this method: using gross rent multipliers derived from sales of dissimilar properties and double counting.

What is wrong with using gross rent multipliers derived from sales of

EXAMPLE OF DEVELOPMENT AND USE OF GROSS RENT MULTIPLIERS

1. Find Typical GRM's Reflected in Recent Sales of Similar Properties:

Apartment project	Sale price	Gross annual ÷ rent roll	Indicated = GRM	Comments on comparison with subject project
Lakeview Apts.	$600,000	$76,956	7.8	Similar units, rented on similar basis
Shamrock Courts	480,000	59,280	8.1	Similar units, rented on similar basis
Regency Villas	250,000	30,480	8.2	Similar units, rented on similar basis
Redwood Apts.	575,000	66,840	8.6	This sale involved purchase-money mortgage very favorable to purchaser. Est. 5 to 10% lower GRM for subject
Terrace Apts.	500,000	68,400	7.3	More utilities furnished by landlord in this case. Est. 10% higher GRM for subject.

2. Use This Information to Value the Subject Property:

Gross Rent Roll for Subject Apartments	$60,000
GRM Indicated by Above Analysis	× 8
Estimated Market Value of Subject Apartments	$480,000

3. And Convert the Estimate of Market Value to a Fair Assessed Value:
   If the required (legal) assessment ratio in your area is 100% but similar properties are typically assessed at ⅔ of market value (the de facto level), then a fair assessment on your property should be on the order of (²/₃ of $480,000) $320,000

properties unlike the property you are appraising? A clear answer to this was included in the ADL report:

> The gross rent multiplier is the market value of a property divided by its annual gross rental receipts. Where variable gross rent multipliers are used, these may provide a reliable rule-of-thumb as to market value. For instance, new luxury apartments may be valued at 7 times gross rents and old blighted properties at 2 times, because these are gross rent multipliers which market prices in fact imply. . . . If the market's gross rent multipliers for luxury and blighted properties are 7 and 2 respectively, but the Assessor's Office applied a uniform multiplier of 5, then luxury buildings must be under-assessed and blighted buildings over-assessed. In order to ensure that this does not happen, however, the assessor must determine what is the appropriate gross rent multiplier for a variety of different structure types and neighborhood conditions. This of course requires the application of one of the appraisal techniques . . . such as the review of sales of comparable properties.

Whenever assessors use gross rent multipliers, there is a danger of double counting—that is, of valuing the same item of property more than once—or of valuing items that are not taxable at all. For example, let's say an apartment is rented with appliances and drapes for $200 per month (or $2,400 per year), and the assessor multiplies $2,400 by a gross rent multiplier. Since part of the rent is imputable to the appliances and drapes, what the assessor did is wrong if these other items are separately assessed as personal property or if they are normally not valued as part of the real estate.

SALE OF THE SUBJECT PROPERTY ITSELF

If you just bought a property in the open market for $25,000, it is hard for an assessor or a review board to maintain that it is worth more. *Hard, but not impossible.* Such a sale can be very persuasive market data, but do not rely on it alone in making a challenge. It is better to be able to prove that this one sale was not a fluke, that it was indeed reasonably consistent with value. And for that you need more data.

ADJUSTING TO THE DE FACTO LEVEL OF ASSESSMENT

Whatever means you use to estimate (full) market value, remember that you then need to reduce this appraised value to the level of taxable value in your jurisdiction. And here the most important standard is *not* the level of assessment required by law. Rather, it is the *actual* level of assessed value that is typical in your area.

Take an example. Let's say a single-family dwelling in Texas is worth $40,000. The law says the property should be assessed at its full value: $40,000. However, if other dwellings in the same area are *actually* typically assessed at, say, 18 percent of full value (as one study found to be about the average in Texas in 1971), then the assessed value should be about $7,200.

How do you find out what this typical level of assessment is in your area? If you are making some use of the market data approach, you already have some information on several sales of similar properties in the area. Find out the assessed value of each of these comparables, divide it by the sale price, and you find the de facto level of assessment in that case. Do this for enough similar properties and you will find out what is typical.

In some areas, such information is already assembled and available; assessment ratio studies have been made and published. If properly done and intelligible (histograms, regression indices, and cumulative condition indicators may obscure the relatively simple information you want), such studies can be helpful.

Supplement C

How to Use the Income Approach

Not one assessment worker in ten has mastered the income approach.

This despite the fact that income properties are a large part of the property tax base. And despite the fact that the people who most often use the formal appeal procedures are the owners of income properties.

Discussion of the income approach here is limited to demonstrating two very useful techniques. Both of these techniques can be used to test the fairness of existing assessments and to project fair assessments for new properties not yet assessed.

THE TAX BURDEN AS A PERCENTAGE OF RENTS

For several types of income properties, the real estate tax burden is the largest single item of operating expense. One meaningful way to compare tax burdens from one income property to another is this: What percentage of the gross rent roll is claimed by the real estate taxes in each case?

Now if this sort of comparison is to be valid, one should confine it to properties which are very similar. And even then, one needs to be alert to individual property differences.

A work-up like the accompanying summary, *"Sundown Apartments: How Fair is the Real Estate Tax Burden as a Percentage of Rents?,"* can help one spot an inequity—and can help get it corrected.

In some cases, it is useful to see how the expenses of your income property stack up against those of other properties of the same type which are sampled in nationwide studies. For example, if you have an unfurnished garden apartment project, you might like to see how your real estate tax burden (as well as other operating items) compares with the real estate

93

SUNDOWN APARTMENTS: HOW FAIR IS THE REAL ESTATE TAX BURDEN AS A PERCENTAGE OF RENTS?

Notes on this comparison: All seven projects are garden apartment projects and are located in Cascade County. All were completed since 1968. In these projects, rents per unit per month range from $165 to $250. Most are rented unfurnished, without heat, and without unusual recreational facilities. (Adjustments were for the exceptions after interviews with the managers.) As a percentage of the rent roll, the real estate tax burden on the Sundown Apartments is clearly unusual and excessive.

	Six Competitive Apartment Projects		
	Colonial Square	*Williamsburg Apartments*	*Woodcrest Villas*
Gross rent roll	$157,500	$120,000	$117,360
Less adjustments for different rental bases:			
Heat included			
Golf course memberships included			
Furnishings in units		48,000	
Gross rent roll on comparable basis	$157,500	$ 72,000	$117,360
Real estate taxes (actual, as of 9/1)	$ 19,367	$ 9,362	$ 11,490
Taxes as % of adjusted gross rent roll	**12.3%**	**13.0%**	**9.8%**

	Brookwood Manor	Forest Hills Apartments	Kensington Apartments	Subject Sundown Apartments
	$337,020	$225,000	$189,000	$234,960
	22,020		9,000	
	9,000			
	$306,000	$225,000	$180,000	$234,960
	$ 36,725	$24,623	$19,440	$46,530
	12.0%	**10.9%**	**10.8%**	**19.8%**

tax burden in generally similar properties across the nation, in your region, and perhaps in your state and city. Some of the major studies:

Shopping centers: *Dollars & Cents of Shopping Centers* is published every three years by ULI (the Urban Land Institute), 1200 18th Street, N.W., Washington, D.C., 20036.

Apartments, condominiums, and cooperatives:

Income/Expense Analysis is published anually by the Institute of Real Estate Management of the National Association of Realtors®, 155 East Superior Street, Chicago, Illinois 60611.

Office buildings: *Office Building Experience Exchange Report* is published each year by the Building Owners and Managers Association International, 224 South Michigan Avenue, Chicago, Illinois 60604.

Motels: An "Annual Motel Financial Report" appears in each July issue of the *Motel/Motor Inn Journal.* Publisher: Tourist Court Journal Co., Inc., 306 East Adams Avenue, Temple, Texas 76501.

Hotels, motor hotels: *Lodging Industry* is published annually by Laventhol & Horwath, 1845 Walnut Street, Philadelphia, Pennsylvania 19103.

A SHORTCUT FOR PROFESSIONALS

The assessment on a neighborhood shopping center is being appealed. The real estate expert retained by the owner has just presented this summary of his estimate of the property's market value:

Real Estate Tax Burden on Subject Property
"True value" of $800,000 × assessment ratio of
   50% × tax rate of 0.1050 = $ 42,000 per annum

Projected Income and Expense in Typical Year

Gross rent roll		$121,000
Less allowance for vacancy and rent loss		6,000
Balance, total operating receipts		$115,000
Real estate taxes	$42,000	
Insurance	2,500	
Maintenance and housekeeping	9,000	
Administrative and miscellaneous	6,500	60,000
Operating balance (before depreciation and debt service)		$ 55,000

Estimate of Market Value

Operating balance of $55,000 ÷ overall capitalization rate of 11% = $500,000

The expert has supported his figures very convincingly, and the Review Board members agree that the income and expenses he has projected and the capitalization rate are all quite reasonable.

Then one of the board members, a bright student of appraising, sees a problem: "All right, the present assessment *does* look too high, but if we reduce the taxes, your expenses will go down, your net income will go up, and so your value estimate will go up—well over $500,000, won't it? I guess what we need to know is how we can get a value and a tax burden that are consistent with each other. How can we do that?"

Here is a direct method to provide the answer to such a question.

    A. Develop a projection of income and expenses as usual . . . with this exception: Do not deduct the real estate tax burden.

    B. Select an overall capitalization rate as usual. To it add the effective tax rate. (This is figured by multiplying the official tax rate by the assessment ratio.)

USING THE INCOME APPROACH TO ESTIMATE THE FAIR ASSESSMENT

Method

· *Effective gross income:*

Start with the possible gross income a well-informed person would anticipate in the typical year in the near future.

Deduct an allowance for anticipated vacancy and rent loss.

Balance, total operating receipts.

· *Less operating expenses* (*except for real estate taxes*):

Insurance

Maintenance and housekeeping

Administrative and miscellaneous

· *Balance: net operating income* (*except for real estate taxes*)
· The final step:

Translate (capitalize) this stabilized income figure into an estimate of market value.

One adds two rates . . .

Overall capitalization rate indicated by market data

The effective tax rate (official tax rate × assessment ratio)

Sum

. . . and then divides the net operating income figure by this sum.

Round the value estimate to a figure that does not tend to overstate the order of precision in your work.

· *Check.*

· *Then, any assessment substantially over this amount would appear too high:*

Estimated market value × assessment ratio = estimated fair assessment

Example

$121,000
  6,000
$115,000

$2,500
 9,000
 6,500

              18,000
            $ 97,000

(0.1050 × 50%)   11.00%
                            5.25%
                           16.25%
($97,000 ÷ 16.25%) $596,923

                          $600,000

If assessor used this value, then tax burden would drop to $31,500 per annum, operating balance (after payment of this tax) would increase to $65,500, and the value estimate would increase to ($65,500 ÷ 11% = $595,455, say) $600,000.

$600,000 × 50% = $300,000

    C. Simply divide the stabilized "net" income estimated in Step A
       by the composite rate developed in Step B.

This long-recognized (if not widely-known) procedure is demonstrated for you in detail on the last two pages.

    A very important point: In computing the effective tax rate, it is usually better to use the *effective* assessment ratio instead of the *"required"* assessment ratio, as demonstrated at the end of the preceding chapter.

ADMINISTRATION

Legal Basis for Assessed Value of Realty, by State: 1975

State	Basis
State	*Basis*
Alabama	Fair and reasonable market value. Effective in 1972, the following percentages thereof apply for the types of realty indicated: Class 1, utilities used in business—30 percent (except in eight counties, where the level is 35 percent). Class 2, property not otherwise classified—25 percent. Class 3, agricultural, forest, and residential—15 percent.
Alaska	Full and true value.
Arizona	Full cash value. Effective January 1, 1974, the following percentages apply for the types of realty indicated: Class 1, flight property, railroads, producing mines—60 percent. Class 2, property of other public utilities—50 percent. Class 3, commercial and industrial property—27 percent. Class 4, all agricultural realty—18 percent. Class 5, residential—15 percent.
Arkansas	20 percent of true and full or actual value.
California	25 percent of fair market value, or of authorized alternate value standard prescribed by state constitution, or by constitutionally authorized statute, and implemented accordingly (e.g., special provisions for property owned by a local govern-

See footnotes at end of table.

State	Basis
	ment but located elsewhere). Fair market value or its authorized alternate is known as "full value."
Colorado	30 percent of actual value.
Connecticut	Not exceeding 100 percent of true and actual or fair market value. A 1974 law (effective May 30) provides that all municipalities must assess at a uniform rate of 70 percent of present true and actual value, adopting same no later than close of next required revaluation. Revaluation is required once every 10 years.
Delaware	True value in money.
District of Columbia	Full and true value in lawful money.
Florida	Full cash value ("just valuation" per state constitution).
Georgia	40 percent of fair market value, effective January 1, 1973.
Hawaii	70 percent of fair market value.
Idaho	20 percent of market value.
Illinois	Fair cash value, which is 50 percent of actual value, except in counties of 200,000 or more which classify property (effective 1971). In any county which classifies, the highest classification may not be more than 2 1/2 times the lowest classification.
Indiana	Just valuation, defined by State as 33 1/3 percent of true cash value.
Iowa	As of January 1, 1975, 100 percent of actual value. Prior standard, 27 percent of actual value.
Kansas	30 percent of fair market value in money.
Kentucky	Fair cash value.
Louisiana	Actual cash value, but each parish authority fixes its assessment level based thereon. New constitution provides for assessment at the following percentages of fair market value, for classifications of property as specified, effective January 1, 1978: Land—10 percent of fair market value.

See footnotes at end of table.

State	Basis

Improvements for residential purposes—10 percent of fair market value.
Agricultural, horticultural, marsh- and timberland—10 percent of use value.
Other property—15 percent of fair market value.

Maine — Just value.

Maryland — Full cash value, i.e., current value less an allowance for any inflation that exists.

Massachusetts — Fair cash valuation.

Michigan — 50 percent of true cash value.

Minnesota — Percentages of market value, as shown (dollar amounts refer to market value):

Homestead—agricultural, first $12,000[1] at 20 percent; excess at 33 1/3 percent. Nonagricultural, first $12,000[1] at 25 percent; excess at 40 percent. Of paraplegic or blind veteran, first $24,000[1] at 5 percent; excess at 33 1/3 percent if agricultural, 40 percent if nonagricultural.

Housing for elderly, others of specified incomes, financed under Title II of National Housing Act, or by Minnesota Housing Finance Agency; for 15 years from construction or rehabilitation, land at 40 percent; structures (in cities, population 10,000 or more, at 20 percent; less than 10,000, at 5 percent).

Nonhomestead—agricultural, at 33 1/3 percent. Residential, at 40 percent.

Apartments, with specified fire-resistant materials, 5 stories or more, at 25 percent; 4 stories or less, at 33 1/3 percent.

Realty for seasonal or temporary use, per days of use in preceding year—200 days or less, at 33 1/3 percent; more than 200 days, at 43 percent.

Timberland, at 20 percent.

Tools, implements, and machinery affixed to public utility realty, at 33 1/3 percent.

Parking ramp structures in first class cities of

See footnotes at end of table.

State	Basis
	400,000 population or less, in 1975, at 36 percent; in 1977, at 43 percent. Petroleum refineries, at 43 percent. Unmined iron ore, at 50 percent. "Low recovery" iron ore, at 30 to 48 1/2 percent. All other realty (including commercial, industrial, public utility), at 43 percent.
Mississippi	Cash value ("in proportion to its value" per state constitution).
Missouri	Effective December 31, 1974, 33 1/3 percent of true value in money.
Montana	Percentages of full cash value, as shown: Realty, except as otherwise provided, at 30 percent.[2] New industrial property, as specified, including pollution control facilities, at 7 percent.[2] Property of electric and telephone cooperatives, at 7 percent. Owner-occupied residence (including affixed mobile home) of a totally disabled veteran, at 7 percent.[2] Widows, widowers, specified retired persons, at 15 percent (up to market value of $27,500). Energy-saving realty, at annual rates increasing from 6 percent to 30 percent.[2,3] Operating property of public utilities, and all property not defined in other separate classifications, at 40 percent.[2]
Nebraska	35 percent of actual value.
Nevada	35 percent of full cash value.
New Hampshire	Full and true value in money.
New Jersey	True value. Taxable value is that percentage of true value, not lower than 20 percent or higher than 100 percent (the particular level being a multiple of 10), as is established by each county board of taxation.
New Mexico	Taxable value not to exceed 33 1/3 percent of value.

See footnotes at end of table.

State	Basis
New York	Full value.
North Carolina	True value in money.
North Dakota	50 percent of true and full value (for most property).
Ohio	Taxable value, not to exceed 50 percent of true value in money.
Oklahoma	Not greater than 35 percent of fair cash value for the highest and best use for which such property was actually used, or was previously classified for use, during the calendar year next preceding the first day of January on which the assessment is made.
Oregon	100 percent of true cash value, i.e., market value as of assessment date.
Pennsylvania	Actual value; but in fourth- to eighth-class counties, not to exceed 75 percent of actual value.
Rhode Island	Full and fair cash value, or a uniform percentage not exceeding 100 percent.
South Carolina	True value in money.
South Dakota	60 percent of true and full value in money.
Tennessee	Classification, effective January 1, 1973: Public utilities.....................................55 percent Industrial and commercial...............40 percent Farm and residential..........................25 percent
Texas	True and full value in money ("in proportion to its value" and never at a value "greater than its fair cash value" per state constitution).
Utah	30 percent of reasonable fair cash value.
Vermont	Listed value which is 50 percent of appraisal value (the latter is fair market value).
Virginia	Fair market value.
Washington	100 percent of true and fair value in money, effective January 1, 1974.
West Virginia	True and actual value, but for classes of property,

See footnotes at end of table.

State	*Basis*
	each subject to a specified rate limit as follows, amounts per $100 of assessed value: I (personalty)—50 cents. II (owner-occupied residential property, including farms)—$1.00. III (all property outside municipalities, other than I and II)—$1.50. IV (all property inside municipalities, other than I and II)—$2.00.
Wisconsin	Full value which could ordinarily be obtained for the property at private sale.
Wyoming	Fair value in conformity with values and procedures prescribed by State Department of Revenue.

[1] Particular amounts in effect as of January 1, 1975. Annual adjustment via index to occur with implementation of 1975 legislative action.
[2] Assessed value at 40 percent of legal standard specified, by statute beginning in 1975 (formerly by regulation).
[3] Effective July 1, 1975.

Actual Assessment Levels on Dwellings Compared with Legal Standards: 1971

State	Ratio of assessed value to sales price[b] (%)	Level (%)	Legal assessment standard[a] Valuation concept	Ratio of actual level to legal standard (%)
(Full-value-standard states)				
Oregon	87.1	100	True cash value	87.1
Kentucky	83.8	100	Fair cash value	83.8
Alaska	75.1	100	Full and true value in money	75.1
New Hampshire	65.1	100	Full and true value in money	65.1
Florida	63.2	100	Full cash value	63.2
Maine	52.9	100	At just value in compliance with the laws of the state	52.9
Massachusetts	49.3	100	Fair cash valuation	49.3
Maryland	47.8	100	Full cash value less an allowance for inflation	47.8
District of Columbia	47.5	100	Full and true value in lawful money	47.5
Wisconsin	46.7	100	Full value at private sale	46.7
Delaware	36.5	100	True value in money	36.5
West Virginia	36.2	100	True and actual value	36.2
Virginia	34.8	100	Fair market value	34.8
New Mexico	27.5	100	Assessed in proportion to its value	27.5

See footnotes at end of table.

State	Ratio of assessed value to sales price[b] (%)	Level (%)	Legal assessment standard[a] Valuation concept	Ratio of actual level to legal standard (%)
Pennsylvania	26.6	100[c]	Actual value (the price for which the property would sell)	26.6
New York	25.8	100	Full value	25.8
Missouri	23.1	100	True value in money	23.1
Texas	18.0	100	Full and true value in money	18.0
Mississippi	14.7	100	Assessed in proportion to its value	14.7
South Carolina	4.0	100	True value in money	4.0
(Fractional-value-standard states)				
Tennessee	32.6	35	Actual cash value	93.1
Georgia	35.7	40	Fair market value	89.2
Iowa	23.3	27	Actual value	86.3
Michigan	41.5	50	Full cash value	83.0
California	20.0	25	Full cash value	80.0
Nebraska	27.5	35	Required to be valued at its actual value and assessed at 35%	78.6
Nevada	27.1	35	Full cash value	80.0
Hawaii	54.0	70	Fair market value or a percentage thereof	77.1
Illinois	37.8	50[d]	Fair cash value	75.6
Ohio	36.9	Up to 50[e]	True value	73.8
Washington	36.1	50	True and fair value	72.2
Kansas	21.3	30	Fair market value	71.0
Indiana	23.5	33 1/3	True cash value	70.6
Colorado	20.7	30	Actual value	69.0
Alabama	19.7	30	Fair and reasonable market value	65.7
Arkansas	12.5	20	True market value in money	62.5
South Dakota	36.5	60	True and full value in money	60.8
Arizona	10.7	18[f]	Full cash value	59.4
Idaho	10.6	20	Market value	53.0
Oklahoma	18.2	35	Fair cash value	52.0
Utah	14.9	30	Reasonable fair cash value	49.7
North Dakota	15.1	50	Full and true value in money	30.1

See footnotes at end of table.

State	Ratio of assessed value to sales price[b] (%)	Legal assessment standard[a]		Ratio of actual level to legal standard (%)
		Level (%)	Valuation concept	
Minnesota	8.5	30[g]	Market value	28.3
Montana	7.7	30[h]	True and full value	25.7

(Varying valuation—determined locally)

Connecticut	47.8	Up to 100	Uniform % of market value within local district	
Louisiana	13.1	Not below 25	Actual cash value (land at not less than $1 per acre)	
New Jersey	58.3	20/100[i]	Uniform percentage at true value	
North Carolina	44.6	[j]	True value in money	
Rhode Island	50.5	[j]	Full and fair cash value	
Vermont	33.3	Up to 100[j]	Fair market value	

(Value determined by state tax commission)

Wyoming	16.6	[k]	Fair value	

[a] The "Legal Standard" rates shown are applicable generally. There are numerous exceptions in several states.

[b] Aggregate assessment—sales price ratio. Residential single-family property.

[c] In fourth- to eighth-class counties, real property must be assessed at a predetermined ratio not to exceed 75 percent.

[d] "Fair cash value" is defined as 50% of the actual value of real and personal property, except in counties of more than 200,000 where real property is classified for tax purposes.

[e] State Board of Tax Appeals authorized to set a fraction for statewide application. In 1972, this fraction was set at 35 percent.

[f] Legal standard varies from 18 to 60 percent depending on class of property.

[g] Estimated. Legal standard varies by class of property. Residential homesteads are assessed at 25% on first $12,000 of market value, 40% on excess.

[h] Legal standard varies from 1–100% depending on class of property.

[i] In a multiple of 10 established by each county board of taxation. If a county fails to establish a uniform percentage, 50% level is employed until action is taken.

[j] Uniform percentage, determined locally.

[k] At a fair value in conformity with values and procedures prescribed by the State Tax Commission.

SOURCE: Advisory Commission on Intergovernmental Relations staff compilation based on data from Commerce Clearing House, *State Tax Reporter;* and U.S. Bureau of the Census, Governments Division.

How Your Assessor Is Selected

In late 1972, a Senate subcommittee sent a questionnaire to all 50 states and the District of Columbia. Among the questions:

(a) Are local property tax assessors in your State elected or appointed?
(b) Are they required to meet any professional qualifications?

Responses were received from all but one (Connecticut).

ALABAMA

Local tax assessors are elected. They are not required to have any professional qualifications.

ALASKA

Local assessors are appointed by the chief executive of the municipality.

ARIZONA

The county tax assessors are the only local assessors in Arizona, and they are not required to meet any professional qualifications.

ARKANSAS

In Arkansas the county assessor serves as the appraiser and assessor for all taxing units—county, city, and school districts. The assessor is elected for a 2-year term. The election laws do not require any educational or technical qualifications.

113

CALIFORNIA

Elected—No.

However, the appraisers, whom the assessor supervises, must pass an examination and be certified by the State.

COLORADO

There are 63 counties in Colorado. In 62 of the counties the county assessor is elected. . . . As to the elected assessors, the only requirement for office is that they obtain more votes than their opponent. In the city and county of Denver the assessor is appointed by the manager of revenue. The appointment may be based on merit, or it may be based on political motivation.

DELAWARE

Appointed. They do not have to meet any professional qualifications as such. There is substantial on-the-job training in each county.

DISTRICT OF COLUMBIA

The administration of the property tax, as well as most other District taxes, is carried out by the Department of Finance and Revenue. The Department Director is an appointed official.

FLORIDA

County tax assessors are elected for 4-year terms; professional qualification requirements have not yet been established.

GEORGIA

Local assessors are appointed by the governing authority of the county. Effective January 1, 1973, assessors must meet minimum qualifications. They must be not less than 25 nor more than 72; they must have 1-year's experience or complete a 40-hour course; they must have a high school diploma or its equivalent; they must successfully complete an assessor certification examination or successfully complete a 40-hour certification course; they must complete at least 40 hours of course work each 2 years they serve.

HAWAII

The department of taxation, which administers all tax programs in the State, is headed by a director who is appointed by the Governor. Within this department, there is a tax assessor in each of the four tax districts (the boundaries of these districts coincide with that of the four counties in the State). These assessors are civil servants and are selected through the State civil service system. Job requirements, relating to experience and education, are set up by the State department of personnel services.

IDAHO

Elected. No.

ILLINOIS

In 100 counties in Illinois the supervisor of assessments—township counties—or county assessor—nontownship counties—is appointed by the county board form a list of persons who have passed an examination given by the Illinois department of local government affairs. Those persons must possess the minimum professional qualifications prescribed by statute. In one county, the county assessor is an elected official. In the remaining county, a five-member board of assessors is elected. In township counties, the township assessor is an elected officer. There are no required qualifications for the elected assessing officials.

INDIANA

Local (township and county) assessors are elected and, like virtually all elected officials, are required to meet no professional qualifications.

IOWA

(a) Appointed by local conference board after qualifying by written examination conducted by director of revenue.
(b) Statutory requirement that only qualified electors of the State shall be eligible to take the assessor examination.

KANSAS

County assessors in Kansas are elected in some counties, generally the more populous ones, and appointed in others. In many counties, the elected county clerk also serves as county assessor.

KENTUCKY

Property valuation administrators who make the assessment for State purposes are locally elected in the counties in which they serve. Before any person's name shall be placed on the ballot he must hold a valid certificate issued by the Department of Revenue showing that he has been examined by it and is qualified to serve. There are no other qualifications other than being a resident of the county and at least 24 years of age.

LOUISIANA

We have 70 assessors in the State and they are elected for 4-year terms.

MAINE

Local assessors in this State may be either elected or appointed. They are not required to meet any professional qualifications.

MARYLAND

For the 23 counties and Baltimore City, the chief assessor is the supervisor of assessments, and his technical staff of appraisers are designated as assessors. There are no stated statewide requirements to meet any professional qualifications. All local governments have been encouraged to establish minimum entrance examinations. (a) Supervisors of assessments are appointed by the director of the State department of assessments and taxation from a list of five nominees submitted by the local government, except in Baltimore City, where the appointment is by the mayor of the city, after consultation with the director of the State department of assessments and taxation. (b) Assessors are nominated, according to State or local laws, by the local governments. They are examined and graded as to their qualifications by this department, and appointment to the position is made, according to State and local laws, by the local governing body. Once appointed, supervisors and assessors can only be removed from office by the State department of assessments and taxation for incompetency or other cause.

MASSACHUSETTS

Generally appointed in cities and elected in towns. No qualifications.

MICHIGAN

1. Assessing officers of townships are the elected township supervisors, number 1,247. There are 264 cities and the assessing officers are in almost all instances appointed. In four cities the assessing officer is elected.

2. The statutes do not provide for professional qualifications. It is safe to assume, however, that in cities where civil service systems are in effect professional qualifications are required of those serving in assessing offices.

3. As of December 31, 1972, all assessors will be required to have been certified as qualified by the State assessors board. As of this writing 45 percent have received the certificate.

MINNESOTA

Property tax assessors are appointed. Under the terms of a 1971 law, all assessors employed by public bodies after December 1, 1974, must be certified as qualified by a State Board of Assessors created by the same law.

MISSISSIPPI

(a) Elected.
(b) No professional qualifications required.

MISSOURI

The local property tax assessors in second-, third-, and fourth-class counties in the State of Missouri are elected. In the two first-class counties, under charter forms of government, and in St. Louis City (not within a county), assessors are appointed. The qualifications are listed in section 82.560, RSMo., 1969, for charter city assessors. With respect to the qualifications for assessor in St. Louis County, a first-class charter county, they do require professional knowledge and actual experience in assessing procedures, as well as technical knowledge involving construction methods and procedures. We believe that here the assessor is primarily an administrator over a sizable group of people who do on-the-spot assessing. We do not have any current information on Jackson County which very recently went under a charter form of government.

MONTANA

(a) Elected at the county level.
(b) No.

NEBRASKA

Nebraska has the county assessor system with 93 assessors. All assessors are elected. Before assuming the office of assessor, the individual must hold an assessor's certificate issued by the tax commissioner. This certificate is based upon the completion of an examination. This law has been tested and upheld by the Nebraska Supreme Court. At the present time, the test could not be described as difficult. Statutory citation: section 77–1326, R.R.S. 1943.

NEVADA

(a) Elected for 4-year terms.
(b) No.

NEW HAMPSHIRE

Local property tax assessors are elected in the 221 towns and appointed in the 13 cities. There are no professional qualifications required in the towns. Several of the cities employ and appoint to their board of assessors appraisers with professional qualifications.

NEW JERSEY

Some New Jersey tax assessors are elected while others are appointed.

Chapter 44, laws of 1967 provides that any assessor appointed or elected after July 1, 1971, must hold a qualified assessor certificate. The division of taxation holds semiannual examinations for qualified applicants.

NEW MEXICO

(a) Elected.
(b) No.

NEW YORK

Each city or town in New York State is required to have a single appointed assessor except as follows:

(a) Any city or town which has exercised an option to have an elected assessor or an elected board of assessors.
(b) Any city or town in a county having the power to assess property for purposes of taxation. (There are two counties which have the power to assess property for purposes of taxation. One such county has a single appointed assessor and the other has an elected board of assessors.)
(c) Cities with a population of 100,000 or more as of the 1970 Federal census.
(d) Villages, most of which copy the assessment roll of the town in which they are located.

Of the 919 towns which have the function of assessing property for tax purposes, 475 have exercised the option to have elected assessors. Six of the 56 cities covered by this requirement have exercised their option to have elected assessors. (See sec. 1522 of article 15-A of the real property tax law. . . .)

Except as noted above, all local assessors are required to meet minimum qualifications established by the State Board of Equalization and Assessment. . . .

NORTH CAROLINA

(a) Appointment for a 2-year term.
(b) No.

NORTH DAKOTA

Local property tax assessors are elected in townships and appointed in the cities. They are not required by law to meet any professional qualifications.

OHIO

Local property tax assessors in Ohio are the county auditors, who are elected for terms of 4 years. There are no professional qualification requirements for these positions.

OKLAHOMA

There are 77 county assessors in Oklahoma, one for each county. They are elected for 2-year terms. They are not required to meet any professional qualifications.

OREGON

The only property tax assessors Oregon has are county assessors. County assessors are elected for 4-year terms unless the county has a home rule charter. Currently, Oregon has five home rule counties, but with two requiring the assessor to be elected. Candidates for the office of county assessor are not required to meet any professional qualifications. Bills have been, and will be again, introduced before the 1973 legislature requiring some qualifications.

PENNSYLVANIA

Tax assessment is under the control of a county board of assessors which is appointed by the county commissioners and except in the largest counties may be the county commissioners themselves. The board of assessment appoints a county assessor. Local assessors are elected in the boroughs and townships while cities either use county assessors or appoint assessors of their own. By statute, local assessors collect data and report to the county assessor, although in practice much of this assessment is done by private firms under contract to the county board of assessors, and in many counties the elected officials have very little authority. There are no specific professional qualifications for assessors.

RHODE ISLAND

In nine of Rhode Island's 39 cities and towns the local property tax assessors are elected. In towns where assessors are elected, there are three part-time assessors. The towns which elect assessors are

Burrillville	Richmond
Exeter	Tiverton
Jamestown	Warren
New Shoreham	West Greenwich
Portsmouth	

In the remaining 30 cities and towns there are full-time appointed assessors. Any professional requirements are determined at the local level.

SOUTH CAROLINA

Local property assessors are appointed and they are not required to meet any qualifications.

SOUTH DAKOTA

All assessors are locally appointed, and they need not meet any professional requirements.

TENNESSEE

(a) Elected.

(b) No.

TEXAS

The county tax assessor/collector is elected in all 254 counties of the State. In a very few of the less populous counties, the elected sheriff serves also as the assessor/collector there. Many of the other municipalities have appointed assessor/collectors.

There are no statutory professional qualifications imposed on assessor/collectors.

UTAH

Local county property tax assessors in our State are elected. There are no professional qualifications required for election to this office. (A recent statute prohibits the appraisal of any property having a market value in excess of $2,000 by an appraiser or assessor unless certified by the State Tax Commission.)

VERMONT

Local listers or assessors are elected and there are presently no requirements for meeting any professional standards.

VIRGINIA

(a) For the statutory 4 and 6 year assessments, real estate assessors are selected from among the citizens of the county, or city, by the judge of the court of record to serve in such a capacity. For those localities undertaking annual assessments, the real estate assessors are appointed by and serve at the pleasure of the local governing body.

(b) Local property tax assessors are not required to meet any professional qualifications.

WASHINGTON

The local county assessors are elected and are not required to meet any professional qualifications. Their staff members, however, who appraise real property for tax purposes must be certified by the State.

WEST VIRGINIA

Local property tax assessors, one for each county, are elected to 4-year terms. They are eligible to succeed themselves and by statute are only required to attend schools and training sessions held by the State tax commissioner.

WISCONSIN

The State law provides that unless each town, village, or city makes special provision for the selection of the assessor, he shall be elected. As a result there is a mixture of appointed and elected assessors. The following tabulation shows the result of a 1972 questionnaire to assessors regarding selection:

Type office held—How selected

Category	Number of assessors in group				Percent to state total		
	All	City	Vil.	Town	All	City	Vil. Town[1]
Full time elected	9	8	1	0	1	4	1
Full time appointed	39	34	2	3	2	17	1
Part time elected	1,226	26	203	997	65	13	51
Part time appointed	416	93	121	202	22	45	30
Nonresident assessor	81	29	34	18	4	14	8
Vacancies as of June 1972	6	1	4	1	1	1	1
No Response	95	12	34	49	5	6	8
State total	1,872	203	399	1,270	100	100	100

Note: State law does not require assessors to have any technical or professional qualifications. Those municipalities who have chosen to appoint assessors impose their own professional requirements via civil service examinations or other such procedures.

[1] Copy illegible.

WYOMING

(a) Elected.
(b) No.

The People Who Judge the Initial Appeals: How They Are Selected

In late 1972, a Senate subcommittee sent a questionnaire to all 50 states and the District of Columbia. Among the questions:

(a) Are the local officials who judge initial appeals from property tax assessments elected or appointed?

(b) Do they derive their authority to hear such appeals from the fact of holding other office?

(c) If so, what is the office (e.g., county commissioner), and what is their other involvement in assessment administration?

Responses were received from all but one (Connecticut).

ALABAMA

County boards of equalization fix property values and hear initial protests. Values as finally fixed by county boards of equalization are appealable de-novo to the circuit court of the county where the property is located. A county board of equalization is composed of three members appointed by the Governor for a 4-year term, one from three names submitted by the county governing body, one from three names submitted by the county board of education, and one from three or more names submitted by the municipalities of the county.

ALASKA

The elected assembly or council sits as the Board for Equalization on valuation appeals. The assembly may, however, delegate this power to a board appointed by it for that purpose. AS 29.53.135.

123

ARIZONA

The county assessor and the county board of supervisors judge initial appeals on property tax assessments, and they are elected. They derive their authority to hear such appeals from the fact that they hold office.

ARKANSAS

Local appeal boards—county equalization boards—are empowered to make adjustments in assessments for the benefit of equalization only. Board members are appointed—one-third by the county judge; one-third by the majority of the members of school district boards; and one-third by the majority of elected city and town council members. Board members cannot hold other public offices.

CALIFORNIA

The board of supervisors or their appointees rule on all initial appeals from property tax assessments. They derive their authority to hear such appeals from their holding elective office.

COLORADO

In 62 counties of the State there are three elected county commissioners who are elected for overlapping 4-year terms. Between the second Monday in July and the last working day of July these three men sit as a county board of equalization. As a board of equalization they receive and hear petitions from all persons whose objections or protests have been refused or denied by the county assessor. In the city and county of Denver, the county board of equalization sits during the same period of time and is composed of the president of the city council and four of the mayor's appointed officials.

DELAWARE

Local appeals judges are appointed by each county to a board of assessment review. They do not derive their authority from holding other offices. They are strictly lay people appointed for specific terms. The procedures for property tax review are specified by State statute.

DISTRICT OF COLUMBIA

The Board of Equalization and Review of the District of Columbia is, by law and through reorganization acts, chaired by the Director of the Department of Finance and Revenue. Other members of the Board are appointed by the chairman and presently consist of both public and citizen members. The public members are employees of the Department of

Finance and Revenue. The citizen members are from the private sector, mainly from the real estate field.

FLORIDA

All members of the board of tax adjustment are elected. The chairman of the local governing body appoints three members of the local governing body to membership on the board. Two additional members are designated by the chairman of the school board from members of the school board. The board hears complaints against individual assessments and denials of exemptions from ad valorem taxation. Any decision rendered by this administrative review board is directly appealable to the State circuit court.

GEORGIA

The local board of equalization, effective in each county for 1973, is appointed by the grand jury. Three members and three alternates are chosen to serve for 1 year, and they hear all appeals for that year. This is the only involvement that this board has in the assessment process.

HAWAII

There is no property tax administered at the local government level.

IDAHO

Elected. Yes. County commissioners. Formally set levies for all local tax jurisdictions, based on property valuation and dollar budgets.

ILLINOIS

In 85 of the township counties the chairman of the county board— elected—and two appointed members constitute the board of review. In two township counties, all members of the reviewing board are elected. In the 15 counties not having townships, the board of county commissioners also serves as the board of review. None of the members of reviewing boards have any other duty with reference to assessments.

INDIANA

Initial appeals from property tax assessments are decided in each of Indiana's 92 counties by a five-member county board of review consisting of three elected officials (county assessor, designated as president; county auditor, designated as secretary, and county treasurer) and two freeholders appointed by the judge of the circuit court.

The county assessor has all the statutory powers of the (township) assessor, which include authority granted the county auditor and county treasurer to serve notice of intent to assess any omitted or undervalued property of any taxpayer.

The county auditor maintains all assessment lists, schedules, statements, maps, and other books and paper filed by (township) assessors.

IOWA

(a) Appointed by local conference board.

(b) No.

KANSAS

Local officials judging initial appeals from assessments are elected. They derive authority by virtue of holding the office of county commissioner. In their appeal function, they are referred to as the county board of equalization. They have no other involvement in assessment administration.

KENTUCKY

Members of the local board of supervisors—initial hearing body—are appointed on a staggered basis to 4-year terms by the county judge. They do not hold other offices, meet only at statutorily specified times, are compensated on a per diem basis for days actually in session, have authority to hear appeals only and have no other tax administrative responsibilities.

LOUISIANA

When the assessor has completed his listings of property, the members of the policy jury, who are elected for 4 years, meet as a board of review and hear complaints of the taxpayers. They make recommendations to the tax commission.

MAINE

If the municipality has a single assessor (rather than a board), there may be an appointed board of assessment review.

Otherwise, appeal is generally to the county commissioners, who are elected or, at the option of the taxpayer, directly to the superior court.

Appeals from forest land valuations may be made to a special three-member ad hoc forestry appeal board made up of the Forest Commissioner, ex officio, one member selected by the taxpayer, and one member selected by the local assessors.

MARYLAND

Under Maryland law, the first level of appeal is to the county supervisor of assessments or his designated representative (generally, the assessor who made the field inspection, and estimated the value of the property). The second right of appeal is to the elected county commissioners or county council, as the case may be. In most jurisdictions, the county commissioners or county councils have designated appeal tax courts, who are by law, the final assessing authority in the county. In the case of county commissioners, their involvement in assessment administration extends to approving the supervisor's annual budget for the purposes of clerical personnel, operating expenses of the office, including space and other necessary facilities.

MASSACHUSETTS

Local boards of assessors are both elected and appointed (generally elected in small municipalities, appointed in large). They also serve as administrators of assessments.

MICHIGAN

Boards of review, initial appeal from property tax assessments, in townships are elected. In cities they may be appointed or may hold office as a member of a board of review by reason of some other public office to which they have been elected or appointed; that is, city of Detroit the common council is the board of review.

MINNESOTA

The first review authority is elected. The members of the review board hold the position by virtue of other offices. The office is that of the authority which employs the assessor (town board, city council, county commissioner). The county commissioner hears appeals from lower boards of review.

MISSISSIPPI

(a) Elected
(b) County supervision.
(c) Equalize assessment.

MISSOURI

In second, third, and fourth class counties, appeals from property tax assessments are reviewed by the county board of equalization, which consists of county judges, assessors, county clerk, and county surveyor. All of these offices are elective. In the first class counties and the city of St. Louis, a similar system is employed; however, the reviewing board here consists of appointed officers. They do derive their authority to hear such appeals in most cases from the fact that they hold another office and in some cases, as in the county commissioners and judges, they could be indirectly involved in the assessment administration.

MONTANA

(a) The local appeal bodies (county boards of equalization) are elected.
(b) They are the three county commissioners in each county.
(c) Since the county commissioners establish the property tax mill levy rate, they are involved with administration as well as appeals. In addition, the county commissioners assess all real property. They are placed in the position of hearing appeals on their own assessments in many cases.

NEBRASKA

Assessment appeals are to an elected board who derives their authority from the fact that they are county comissioners. The principal other involvement in assessment administration of the county commissioners, other than hearing appeals, is adopting a budget for the assessor's office and if there is a countywide mass appraisal entering into the contract.

NEVADA

(a) Elected.
(b) Yes.
(c) All county commissioners plus representatives of school board trustees and of each city council within county.
This group sits as the county board of equalization to hear appeals regarding assessment of locally assessed property.

NEW HAMPSHIRE

Local officials (selectmen of towns) judging initial appeals are elected in towns and appointed in cities (city assessor or board of assessors). They derive their authority to hear appeals from the fact of holding office as seselectmen, city assessors or members of the board of assessors. The selectmen of towns and the board of assessors or city assessors in cities assess the initial tax and administer the tax laws on the local level.

NEW JERSEY

(a) Members of county tax board are appointed.
(b) No.

NEW MEXICO

(a) Elected.
(b) Yes.
(c) County commissioner, review assessments.

NEW YORK

Local assessment review boards are appointed. The members of such boards do not serve by virtue of the fact that they hold any office.

NORTH CAROLINA

(a) Elected except in a few counties which have special boards of equalization and review appointed by the board of county commissioners.
(b) Yes.
(c) County commissioners. They must approve schedules of value (unit prices) used in revaluations and must take final action on assessments of discovered property.

NORTH DAKOTA

Local officials who judge initial appeals from property tax assessors are appointed. At the township level, the elected supervisors act as the local board of equalization while at the city and county level, the elected commission or council members act as the board of equalization.

OHIO

At the local level in Ohio, initial appeals from real property assessments are heard by the county boards of revision, which are comprised of three elected officials—county auditor, county treasurer, and president of the board of county commissioners—all of whom sit on the board of revision by virtue of holding other office. Of the three, only the county auditor has any other involvement in property assessment administration; he is the assessor of all real property (except public utility) and is a deputy of the State tax commissioner with respect to personal property assessment. (Personal property assessment appeals are heard first by the State tax commissioner.) Board of revision rulings may be appealed to the State board of tax appeals.

OKLAHOMA

The local officials who judge initial appeals from property tax assessments are appointed. No, they do not derive their authority to hear such appeals from the fact of holding other office. Their other involvements in assessment administration are:

(a) Equalize, correct, and adjust the assessed valuation of real and tangible personal property by raising or lowering the valuation of the property of any taxpayer to conform to the fair cash value thereof, as defined by law.

(b) Add omitted property.

(c) Cancel assessments of property not taxable.

(d) Review homestead exemptions and determine claimants' eligibility.

(e) Approve special revaluation budgets and apportion revaluation costs among the various recipients of ad valorem tax proceeds on a pro rata basis.

OREGON

County boards of equalization consist of three members. One member is a member of the county court or the county board of commissioners, as the case may be. This member is an elected official but appointed by the court or board of county commissioners to serve on the county board of equalization. The second member is appointed from the county budget committee. The third member is a freeholder appointed by the other two members of the board. Thus, the member of the board who is also a member of the county governing body, and the budget member of the board, serve on the county board of equalization by virtue of other offices they hold. Portions of the 1973 manual for boards of equalization explain the circumstances under which the compilation of the board differs from that . . . described.

The county boards of equalization have the responsibility to hear appeals and to equalize the assessment roll. In addition, the boards are required to make recommendations to improve assessments, by not later than December 15 of each year, to the county assessors. The . . . board of equalization calendar and schedule briefly explains the duties of the board throughout the year.

PENNSYLVANIA

Appeals boards are appointed by the county commissioners. They determine the assessments and are the first level of appeal. In many cases, their members are the county commissioners. The board of assessors appoints a county assessor and is responsible for the overall administration of property assessment in each county.

RHODE ISLAND

The boards of review of assessments are appointed for that specific office at the local level.

SOUTH CAROLINA

The local officials who judge the initial appeals are appointed. They do not derive their authority to hear such appeals from the fact of holding other offices.

SOUTH DAKOTA

Local officials are the local board who govern the tax entity, and they are elected officials. Generally, the local board terms are for 2 or 3 years. Our local board of equalization is composed of the members of the local governmental board who are the elected officials of that tax entity. The next appeals board is composed of the county commissioners, who are the county board of equalization and also are elected.

TENNESSEE

(a) Appointed by the county court, or governing legislative body of the local jurisdiction.
(b) No.

TEXAS

At the county level, the elected county commissioners hear initial appeals sitting as the county board of equalization. The commissioners court also determines the budget level of the assessment office which has a significant impact on the level of assessment/collection activities.

Appeals from assessments in municipalities and school districts are heard by boards of equalization appointed by the mayor, city council, and school board of trustees respectively.

UTAH

The local officials who judge initial appeals are the elected county commissioners, of which there are three. When so acting, they are known as the "county board of equalization." They derive their authority to hear such appeals from the fact of holding the commission office. There is pending in the courts the question as to whether the county board of equalization has the authority to exempt property placed on the tax rolls by the assessor. Heretofore, the board has exercised such a jurisdiction.

VERMONT

The first level of appeal is to the local assessors or board of listers, as they are referred to in Vermont. The second step is also to a local jurisdiction known as the board of civil authority, which is composed of the selectmen of the town, the elected justices and the town clerk. All of these persons are locally elected officials of the town. Their authority derives from the holding of their respective offices.

VIRGINIA

Members of boards of equalization of real estate assessments in all localities are primarily appointed by the judge of the court where deeds are admitted to record. Some appointments are, however, made by the governing body. None are elected. None of the appointees hold other local governmental positions.

WASHINGTON

The local officials who judge initial appeals from property tax assessments are the county boards of equalization appointed by the board of county commissioners; or, the commissioners themselves act as the board of equalization. Their only involvement is in the equalization of assessments and hearing appeals from property taxpayers.

WEST VIRGINIA

The local officials who judge initial appeals from property tax assessments in West Virginia are the three commissioners of the county court in each county. These commissioners are elected. County commissioners have an interest in maintaining high assessments because they are also the body that administers county government, and they are vitally interested in the property tax which is their sole source of revenue.

WISCONSIN

In towns the members of the board of review shall be the town supervisor and town clerk; in cities of the first class (Milwaukee) the members of the board of review shall by ordinance consist of five residents of the city none of whom shall occupy any public office or be publicly employed. All cities other than Milwaukee and all villages have the option of appointing (1) a citizens board of review as described above for cities of the first class, or (2) the mayor, the clerk, and such other officers other than assessor, as the common council of each city determines or the president, the clerk, and such other officers other than the assessor as the board of trustees of each village determines.

WYOMING

(a) Elected.
(b) Yes; County Commissioners.
(c) None.

The Members of the State-Level Tax Review Agency: How They Are Chosen

In late 1972, a Senate subcommittee sent a questionnaire to all 50 states and the District of Columbia. Among the questions:

(a) How and by whom are the members of the state-level tax assessment review agency chosen?

(b) What is their term of office?

(c) Does their agency have responsibility for assessing inter-county property, and, if so, what property (e.g., utility, railroad, etc.)?

(d) Do they also supervise local assessment standards and administration?

Responses were received from all but one (Connecticut).

ALABAMA

The department of revenue prior to 1972 had statutory general supervision of the administration of the property tax in all counties, however, historically and for some practical reasons, the assistance given the counties was limited to appraisal assistance by department personnel on request by a county board of equalization. Beginning in 1972 the department of revenue has become active in the direction and supervision of a statewide reappraisal program designed to equalize tax assessments. This policy change was brought about by a court order and an act of the Alabama Legislature directing equalization of property taxes. The act of the legislature further directs the department of revenue to maintain equalization when the in-progress revaluation program has been completed. Assessment of utility and railroad properties are made on a unit basis at the State level.

ALASKA

There is no State-level tax assessment review agency and the State does not assess, levy or collect property taxes on any class of property. The standard of value to be used by municipalities for the purpose of property assessment is prescribed in Alaska statutes as follows:

> Sec. 29.53.060. Full and true value. (a) The assessor of a municipality shall assess property at its full and true value as of January 1 of the assessment year, except as provided in this section and sections 30, 35, and 160 of this chapter. The full and true value is the estimated price which the property would bring in an open market and under the then prevailing market conditions in a sale between a willing buyer and a willing seller both conversant with the property and with prevailing general price levels.

(In the court case, *Hoblit* v. *Greater Anchorage Area Borough* (Sup. Ct. Op. No. 636) the court ruled that the borough has discretion to appraise by whatever recognized method of valuation it chooses, so long as there is no fraud or clear adoption of a fundamentally wrong principle of valuation. In 1963, the Local Affairs Agency, predecessor to the Division of Local Government Assistance, published the "Property Appraisal Manual for Alaska Assessors" which contains recommended methods and standards of appraisal. The methods and procedures as outlined in this manual were generally adopted and used by the various municipalities. In 1970 the agency published the "Residential Appraisal Cost Manual for Alaska Assessors." This manual was a complete revision of the residential section of the original manual. It contained 1970 construction cost data, a wider range of property types, specifications and area adjustment factors.

ARIZONA

The three members of the State level property tax appeals board are appointed for a term of 6 years by the Governor of the State. This board has the responsibility for hearing property tax appeals from decisions at the county level, and for equalizing property valuations throughout the entire State.

ARKANSAS

Arkansas does not have a State-level tax assessment review agency, per se. The tax division of the public service commission does, by special statutes, assess utility and carrier property only. They are not empowered to supervise local assessment standards and administration.

CALIFORNIA

Members of the State board of equalization, all elected officials, serve 4-year terms and hear all appeals where more than one jurisdiction is concerned. The board also hears appeals not settled by the local boards of supervisors. The board assesses public utilities and intercounty pipelines. It allocates the values thus determined among the taxing districts in which the property is located.

COLORADO

The answer to this question will be divided into two parts:

(a) A new agency in Colorado is the Board of Assessment Appeals. This is a three-man board appointed by the Governor for overlapping 6-year terms. If a county board of equalization denies the petition of the taxpayer, the taxpayer may appeal to the Board of Assessment Appeals no later than 30 days after such denial. The Board of Assessment Appeals came into existence by legislative act July 1, 1971.

(b) Division of Property Taxation—The head of the Division of Property Taxation is the Property Tax Administrator who is appointed by the executive director of the Department of Local Affairs subject to the provisions of section 13 of article XII of the State constitution, which means appointment under a merit or civil service-type appointment. The Property Tax Administrator assesses and apportions the value of railroad, airline, electric, rural electric, telephone, telegraph, gas, gas pipeline carrier, domestic water, pipeline, street transportation, sleeping car, express, and private car line companies. He has no authority to assess properties, not enumerated, that operate in two or more counties of the State.

DELAWARE

There is no State-level tax assessment review agency.

DISTRICT OF COLUMBIA

This question is not applicable to the District.

FLORIDA

In Florida there is no State level tax assessment review agency. Railroad and telegraph property is centrally assessed by the ad valorem tax division, department of revenue. This department also is charged with the general supervision of local assessment standards.

GEORGIA

The State board of equalization is comprised of the attorney general, the State auditor, the chairman of the House Ways and Means Committee, the chairman of the Senate Banking and Finance Committee, and the State revenue commissioner. This board has the responsibility for reviewing and approving State assessments on railroad and public utility properties and the assessment of motor vehicle property. They also hear all appeals from railroad and public utility companies regarding property tax assessments. The board has no responsibility for reviewing local assessments, but it does prescribe procedures, etc., by which the local boards of equalization conduct hearings, etc.

HAWAII

A board of review in each tax district constitutes the initial level of the appeal process in Hawaii. Each board consists of five members who are appointed by the Governor. Board members must be residents of the district for which the board is appointed and must have resided in the State for at least 3 years prior to the time of the appointment. An officer or employer of the State is not eligible for appointment to the board. The term for each appointment is 4 years; however, a person may serve for two terms but no more.

In regard to the question concerning intercounty property, specifically those owned by utilities and railroads, it should be noted that it does not present a problem in Hawaii. For one thing, utilities are not taxable in Hawaii. Second, being an island State, we are not faced with problems concerning properties overlapping two or more counties.

IDAHO

Governor appoints State Board of Tax Appeals, subject to confirmation of Senate. Term is 3 years. No, this is function of tax commission. No.

ILLINOIS

Appointed by the Governor with the advice and consent of the Senate. Six-year term. The Illinois Property Tax Appeal Board has no direct assessment jurisdiction and does not have authority to supervise local assessment standards and equalization.

INDIANA

The Governor of Indiana appoints the three-member State board of tax commissioners for 4 years, his pleasure or discretion, or until successors are appointed.

Included in its responsibilities is the assessment, by the unit method of valuation, of public utilities, railroads, and private car lines.

The board prescribes rules, regulations, forms, and schedules used for assessment; instructs, assists, and supervises local assessing officials; and construes the property tax laws.

IOWA

(a) By Governor of State subject to confirmation by two-thirds of members of senate.

(b) Six-year term.

(c) No responsibility to assess property.

(d) No. Not directly.

KANSAS

The Governor appoints members of the board of tax appeals to 5-year terms.

The board has review responsibility for local assessment by the counties, for State assessment of motor carriers, and for State appraisal of public utility firms, including telephone, pipeline, electrical, railroad, water, and radio common carriers.

On a review or appellate basis, the board indirectly supervises all assessment administration in Kansas.

KENTUCKY

Responsibility for assessment review lies wholly with the Department of Revenue. This agency supervises local assessments and can reject assessments that do not meet the fair cash value standard or apply equalization increases to the aggregate assessment of any class of property. It also has responsibility for assessment of all corporations, companies, associations, partnerships or persons performing any public service—railroads, utilities, and so forth.

The Commissioner of Revenue is appointed by the Governor and the Director of the Property Division by the Commissioner with approval of the Governor.

LOUSIANA

The Louisiana Tax Commission is composed of a chairman and two members. They are appointed by the Governor to 6-year terms overlapping. This commission reviews the assessments made by the assessors covering all real estate and personal property. All public service property, such as railroads, pipe lines, telephones, etc., is assessed directly by the commission.

MAINE

The State-level assessment review agency is the superior court, whose members are appointed by the Governor for 7-year terms.

Inter-county property is assessed locally, not at the State level.

The State bureau of taxation has general supervision over local assessment administration; but no appellate authority.

MARYLAND

Assessment administration in the 23 counties and Baltimore City is under the control and direction of the State department of assessments and taxation. The director of that department is appointed by the Governor, and the term of office is indefinite, but is subject to mandatory retirement at age 70. Other assessing personnel in the State department of assessments and taxation's central office are charged with the duty of valuing railroad property, property of public utilities, franchise tax of domestic and foreign financial institutions, tangible personal property of foreign and domestic ordinary business corporations, and to provide direct supervision of the local supervisors and assessors in the counties and Baltimore City. Various appraisal aids, such as manuals and tax maps, and training in the appraisal techniques is supplied by the department to all local assessors.

On the State level, there is a Maryland tax court, the third level of appeal from the local assessments, or the second level of appeal from the decision from the director of the State department of assessments and taxation, in the case of assessments made at the state level. The Maryland tax court consists of five judges appointed by the Governor for terms of 6 years.

MASSACHUSETTS

State bureau of local assessment is part of State civil service system. Members must pass examinations; serve until retirement age 65. They value utility property, advise but do not supervise local assessors.

MICHIGAN

Assessment review at the State level is by the State tax commission. It consists of three members appointed by the Governor for a 6-year term. The agency does not have responsibility for assessing intercounty property as such but does have responsibility under another act for assessing utility property, specifically railroad, telephone and telegraph, but not pipeline, electrical transmission and distribution, et cetera. The commission has responsibility for supervising local assessment standards and administration.

MINNESOTA

The State review agency is the State commissioner of taxation, a gubernatorial appointee. The commissioner has the responsibility of equalizing assessment levels between assessing districts. The commissioner can and does order changes when he finds disparities. Yes.

MISSISSIPPI

(a) Have three-man tax commission.
(b) 6-year appointment.
(c) Yes, utility and railroads.
(d) Yes.

MISSOURI

The State level tax assessment review agency in the State of Missouri is the Missouri State Tax Commission. They are appointed by the Governor with the advice and consent of the Missouri Senate. Their term of office is 6 years and the terms are staggered so that one member of the commission is appointed every 2 years. The State Tax Commission does not have responsibility for assessment of intercounty property except that all utility and railroad property is valued by the tax commission at State level with a distribution of value to the counties and political subdivisions involved.

The tax commission has authority to equalize between counties but has little, if any, authority in intercounty assessments except as a final review board.

MONTANA

(a) The three-member State board of equalization is appointed by the Governor.
(b) The members serve overlapping 6-year terms. Not more than two members may be from the same political party.
(c) The State board assesses all intercounty such as railroads, utilities, pipelines, telephone lines, and so forth.
(d) The board also supervises local officials although their powers are limited. They act more in an advisory than in a supervisory capacity.

NEBRASKA

The State-level tax assessment review agency is known as the State board of equalization and assessment. By constitution, the members are the Governor, the Secretary of State, the auditor of public accounts, the State treasurer and the tax commissioner. The term of office is 4 years for the elected members. The tax commissioner serves at the pleasure of the Governor. The state board of equalization has responsibility for valuing railroad properties, car lines and public utility franchises. They do not supervise local assessment standards and administration. This is done by the tax commissioner. The tax commissioner is responsible for central assessment of non-resident bus and trucks and airlines as well as establishing the valuation to be used for motor vehicles and livestock.

NEVADA

(a) Appointed by Governor (members of Nevada Tax Commission).
(b) 4 years (staggered terms).
(c) Yes, all property of all interstate and intercounty railroad, sleeping car, private car, street railway, traction, telegraph, water, telephone, air transport, electric and power companies, together with franchises but excluding motor vehicles.
(d) Yes, establish and monitor standards and procedures.

NEW HAMPSHIRE

The State-level review agency comprising three tax commissioners are appointed by the New Hampshire Supreme Court for terms of 6 years. The intercounty property of electric, gas and oil pipeline companies is assessed locally based on data supplied by these utilities to the selectmen and assessors. The tax commission assesses the property of telephone, telegraph and railroad property at the State level with the taxes retained by the State. The tax commission, by statute, supervises local assessment administration and standards.

NEW JERSEY

(a) Members of the division of tax appeals, Department of Treasury, are appointed by the Governor.
(b) 5 years.
(c) No.
(d) No. Such standards and administration are supervised by the division of taxation, Department of the Treasury, and by the respective county boards of taxation.

NEW MEXICO

(a) Appointed by Governor.
(b) Four years.
(c) Yes; airlines, utilities, railroads, pipelines, water companies, mines, contractors' equipment.
(d) Yes.

NEW YORK

There is no State level administrative assessment review agency. However, the real property tax law does provide for judicial review of assessments by the regular State courts for taxpayers who have availed themselves of the local administrative review.

The State Board of Equalization and Assessment assesses real property in streets and other public places; real property used for transportation purposes of railroad companies subject to the railroad exemption law and those State-owned lands which are taxable pursuant to the provisions of the real property tax law. The State board also has advisory and supervisory functions with respect to local assessment standards and administration.

NORTH CAROLINA

(a) The State board of assessment is a five-member board; two are appointed by the Governor and one each by the Lieutenant Governor and speaker of the house of representatives. The fifth member is the director of the division of tax research of the department of revenue, who serves ex-officio.

(b) The four appointed members are appointed for 4-year terms.

(c) Yes. Railroads and public utilities property, including the rolling stock of trucking companies and bus lines and the flight equipment of airlines.

(d) In law but not in fact.

NORTH DAKOTA

State board of equalization consists of five elected constitutional officers: Governor, State auditor, State treasurer, commissioner of agriculture, and the commissioner of taxation. Terms of service run concurrent with their terms of office, 4 years. The State board of equalization makes utility assessments and has the authority to change local assessments.

OHIO

There are two State level tax review boards in Ohio:

(a) The State tax commissioner hears all initial appeals from public utility and personal property taxes (and all other taxes administered by the tax commissioner). Personnel used in this capacity are full-time civil service employees and, in practice, those dealing with property taxes have been attorneys.

The tax commissioner has responsibility for all policy and assessment standards (using legislatively set assessment levels) and general administration of all tangible personal property taxes, including personal property of intercounty businesses and public utility property. The real property component of public utility property also is a responsibility of the tax commissioner, and represents his only involvement in the area of real property taxes.

(b) The State board of tax appeals (BTA) is the second step in the appeals process having, among its several functions, the hearing of appeals from the county boards of revision and the tax commissioner; BTA hearings are *de novo* proceedings. The BTA is a three-member "tax court" whose members are appointed for staggered 6-year terms by the Governor, subject to senate approval.

Attached to the BTA is an administrative unit, the division of county affairs, which is the State level coordinator of the (local) real property tax. Duties of county affairs include prescribing all property tax forms and reviewing real property appraisal lists to determine whether appraisals are at the required level.

Beyond the BTA, tax appeals progress to the court of appeals or the Ohio Supreme Court.

OKLAHOMA

The State Board of Equalization is the State-level assessment review agency. Its membership is specifically named in the State constitution. The members are

(1) The Governor (elected)
(2) The Attorney General (elected)
(3) The State Treasurer (elected)
(4) The Secretary of State (elected)
(5) The State Examiner and Inspector (elected)
(6) The State Auditor (elected)
(7) The President of the State Board of Agriculture (appointed)

The terms of office of the six members of the State Board of Equalization who are elected to office are for 4 years. The term of office of the president of the Board of Agriculture is 5 years. The State Board of Equalization assesses all property of railroads, utilities, and other public service companies. While the board does not directly supervise local assessment standards and administration, certain limited authority has been statutorily vested in the Oklahoma Tax Commission to advise and assist the county assessors in the performance of their duties.

OREGON

The director of the department of revenue is the sole member of the State-level tax assessment reviewing body. The director is appointed by the Governor and his term of office is 4 years. The department of revenue does have the responsibility for assessing intercounty property. Such centrally assessed property consists of the following companies: airline, electric, express, gas, heating, pipeline, railroad, tank and private car, telegraph, telephone, water, and water transportation.

Yes, the department supervises local assessment standards and administration.

PENNSYLVANIA

There is no State level body which supervises local assessment standards and administration. The State tax equalization board calculates state-wide equalization formulas based on local assessments. These are the basis for State subsidies to local school districts. The State tax equalization board does no assessing of its own.

RHODE ISLAND

There is no State level tax assessment review agency in Rhode Island. However, the tax equalization section of the department of community affairs attempts to fill that gap. Findings by that agency are not used to equalize or adjust local assessments, but are used in computing State aid to education.

SOUTH CAROLINA

The South Carolina Tax Commissioners who are appointed by the Governor for a 6-year term are the State-level tax assessment review agency. The Tax Commission assesses all public utilities, manufacturers, merchants, fixtures, and inventory. The Tax Commission also supervises local assessments.

SOUTH DAKOTA

The State board of equalization is composed of five members who are appointed by the Governor for 3-year terms. They are the final board of appeals for individual assessment grievances and also make the final decision on utility assessments. They may raise or lower county level of assessments, by classes, when appealed by another tax entity, where overlapping school districts require equalization. They may raise or lower any class of property, in any county, where they feel an adjustment is needed, but this adjustment is limited by other criteria that, in fact, makes it more of a nuisance than a value.

TENNESSEE

(a) By law, the State Board of Equalization consists of the Governor, Secretary of State, Comptroller of the Treasury, State Treasurer, and two persons appointed by the Governor with knowledge and experience in city and county government.

(b) Each term of office is as follows:
   Governor, 4 years.
   Secretary of State, 4 years.
   Comptroller of the Treasury, 2 years.
   State Treasurer, 2 years.
   Appointee with experience in city government, 4 years.
   Appointee with experience in county government, 4 years.

(c) They do not have the responsibility of assessing intercounty property although they have the responsibility to review the assessments of such property. This property includes all property assessed by the Public Service Commission, and includes all of the properties belonging to the following persons and companies: (1) railroads; (2) telephones; (3) telegraphs; (4) sleeping cars; (5) freight cars; (6) streetcars; (7) power, whether hydroelectric, steam, or other kinds, for the transmission of power; (8) express; (9) pipelines; (10) gas companies; (11) electric light companies; (12) motor bus and/or truck and (13) water companies.

(d) Yes.

TEXAS

The only State-level tax assessment review agency in Texas is the Intangible Tax Board composed of the State comptroller, the secretary of state, and the State treasurer. The comptroller and the treasurer are elected officials with 2-year terms (due to a constitutional amendment in 1972, those elected terms will be increased to 4 years effective 1974). The secretary of state is appointed to office by the Governor and serves a term running concurrently with that of the Governor (4 years effective 1974). The Intangible Tax Board is responsible for the assessment of ad valorem taxes on the intangible assets of railroads, pipeline companies, and motor carrier companies. The board makes an annual assessment and distributes it to taxing districts for collection on a mileage per district basis. There is no State-level supervision of local assessment standards or administration.

UTAH

The State Tax Commission, a four-member body, operates as a quasi-judicial body in reviewing tax appeals coming up from the local county boards. The authority to hear such appeals is vested under the constitution and statutes. This appeal function applies only to locally assessed property. All mines, utilities, railroads, and gas and oil properties are assessed directly by the State Tax Commission. The supervision of locally assessed property, the setting of standards are an administrative function of the State Tax Commission.

The State Tax Commission and its functions are constitutional. All of the four members, serving an appointed term of 4 years each, are appointed by the Governor and approved by the State Senate. Two members are appointed each biennium, one from each major political party.

VERMONT

Members of the State Tax Appeals Board, three in number, are appointed by the Commissioner of Taxes for a period of 1 year. Two boards conduct appeals onsite throughout the entire State. Such boards have no responsibility for assessing intercounty property, nor do they have any authority with respect to the supervision of local assessment standards or administration.

VIRGINIA

(a) and (b) Virginia does not assist on the State level with the equalization function. The department of taxation upon the request of the locality is required to render assistance to the local board of equalization on the local level. Calendar year in counties—first 6 months in cities.

(c) Virginia's constitution provides for the assessment of public service corporations (e.g., railroads or utility companies with public service charters) by a central State agency. Assessed values are fixed by the State corporation commission and annually certified to the local governmental units. Taxes on such assessed values are extended locally.

(d) There is no direct supervision over local assessment standards and administration.

WASHINGTON

The State board of tax appeals is a three-member panel appointed by the Governor to staggered 6-year terms. The board hears appeals by either taxpayers or county assessors from decisions handed down by the county boards of equalization. The responsibility of assessing intercounty utilities, such as railroads, utility companies, et cetera, rests with the department of revenue. This department also supervises the local assessment practices and procedures.

WEST VIRGINIA

In West Virginia, a county assessor's assessments are not reviewed by a State level agency. Rather, the State tax department performs appraisals on all real property as well as industrial and commercial personal property. These values are certified to the several counties, and the assessor uses these values as a basis for his assessments. An appeal from the county court's review would go to the courts of general jurisdiction—the circuit court and the supreme court of appeals.

The State tax department prepares tentative assessed values for all public utility property in West Virginia. This assessment is reviewed and finalized by the Board of Public Works, a body composed of the several elected executive officers in West Virginia (that is, the Governor, secretary of state, attorney general, State treasurer, State auditor, State agriculture commissioner (and the superintendent of free schools, who is not elected).

The State tax department has some statutory authority to supervise local assessment standards and practices.

WISCONSIN

The State tax appeals commission has limited review powers with respect to property valuation. It reviews the values adopted by a county board used for apportioning the county property tax levy among its constituent municipalities. The commission does not review appeals of individual property owners or the equalized values determined by the State for the apportionment of school levies. The commission consists of three members appointed by the Governor and approved by the senate for staggered 6-year terms. Almost all other State administrative supervisory or review duties with respect to the property tax are vested in the department of revenue. The secretary of the department of revenue serves at the Governor's pleasure. The bureau of property and utility tax within the department of revenue determines the equalized taxable property values of general property as well as the primary values of intercounty property of common carrier except motor transport, heat, light, and power companies and natural gas companies.

WYOMING

(a) Appointed by Governor, confirmed by State Senate.
(b) 6 years.
(c) Yes; i.e. all mineral production including oil, natural gas, railroads, pipelines, telephone and telegraph, and all other public utilities. 1972 assessment was 54 percent of the State total.
(d) Yes.

RELIEF AND EXEMPTIONS

State	Financed by	Date of adoption	Description of beneficiaries (estimated number of claimants)
Alabama	Localities (mandated)	1973	Homeowners 65 and over
	State (exemption applies to state taxes only)	1971	Homeowners 65 and over (na)
Alaska	State	1972 1973 rev.	Homeowners 65 and over (1,000)
Arizona	State (circuit breaker)	1973	Homeowners and renters 65 and over
Arkansas	State (circuit breaker)	1973	Homeowners 65 and over (90,000)
California	State (circuit breaker)	1967 1972 rev.	Homeowners 62 and over (292,999)
	State	1972	All renters (na)
Colorado	State (circuit breaker)	1971 1973 rev.	Homeowners and renters 65 and over (11,000)

Supplement I

Principal State Property Tax Relief Policies for Homeowners and Renters: 1/1/74

Income ceiling	Tax relief formula (or general remarks)	Form of relief (estimated per capita cost)
$5,000	Total exemption.	No tax liability (na)
None	The $2,000 general exemption of assessed value for state ad valorem taxes only is increased to $5,000 for homeowners, 65 and over.	Reduced in tax bill (na)
None	Total exemption.	No tax liability ($1.54)
$3,500 single $5,000 married (value of property not to exceed $5,000)	A percentage of tax is returned as a credit, percentage declines as income rises. Only taxes on first $2,000 of assessed value are considered. (25% of rent = tax equivalent, not to exceed $225)	State income tax credit or rebate
$5,000	Taxes exceeding various percentages of income are remitted; percentages range from 1% on incomes below $1,500 to 5% on incomes above $4,500.	State income tax credit or rebate ($1.39)
$10,000 net $20,000 gross	Relief ranges from 96% of tax payment on first $7,500 of value if net household income is less than $1,400 to 4% of tax payment if net household income is $10,000 (in addition to a state-financed homestead exemption of $1,750 for all homeowners).	State rebate ($2.93)
None	Relief ranges from $25 if adjusted gross income is less than $5,000 to $45 on income of $8,000 and over.	State income tax credit or rebate (na)
$5,400 single $6,300 married (Net worth less than $20,000)	Relief limited to 50% of the tax payment and cannot exceed $270. The credit or refund is reduced by 10% of income over $2,700 for individuals and 10% of income over $3,600 for husband and wife. (10% of rent = tax equivalent).	State income tax credit or rebate ($.32)

151

State	Financed by	Date of adoption	Description of beneficiaries (estimated number of claimants)
Connecticut	State (circuit breaker) [replaces 1965 state-financed program]	1973	Homeowners and renters 65 and over
Delaware	Localities (mandated)	1965 1967 rev.	Homeowner 65 and over (na)
	Localities (optional)	1969 1970 rev.	
Florida	State	1971	Homeowners 65 and over (362,000)
Georgia	Localities (mandated)	1964 1972 rev.	Homeowners 65 and over (100,000)
	Localities (mandated)	1972	Homeowners 62 and over (na)
Hawaii	Localities (mandated)	1969 1972 rev.	Homeowners 60 and over (180,000)
Idaho	Localities (mandated)	1969 1973 rev.	Homeowners 65 and over (na)
Illinois	State (circuit breaker)	1972	Homeowners and renters age 65 and older or disabled (290,000)
	Localities (mandated)	1971	Homeowners 65 and over (na)
Indiana	Localities (mandated)	1957 1971 rev.	Homeowners 65 and over (80,000)
	State (circuit breaker)	1973	Homeowners and renters, 65 and over

Income ceiling	Tax relief formula (or general remarks)	Form of relief (estimated per capita cost)
$7,500	Taxes exceeding 5% of income. Maximum refund ranges up to $500 for incomes below $3,000 (20% of rent = tax equivalent).	Reduction in tax bill
$3,000	Exemption of $5,000 assessed value from state or county property taxes.	Reduction in tax bill (na)
(Same provisions as above, for municipal taxes)		
None	The locally financed general homestead exemption of $5,000 for all homeowners is increased to $10,000 for homeowners 65 and over for taxes levied by district school boards for current operating purposes (state financed).	Reduction in tax bill ($1.47)
$4,000	The general homestead exemption of $2,000 for all homeowners is increased to $4,000 for homeowners 65 and over (additional state financed homestead relief is provided to all homeowners equivalent to a $1,000 exemption).	Reduction in tax bill ($1.48)
$6,000	Exemption of ad valorem taxes for educational purposes levied on behalf of school districts.	Reduction in tax bill (na)
None	The general homestead exemption of $8,000 for all homeowners is increased to $16,000 for homeowners of age 60 to 69.	Reduction in tax bill ($4.40)
	Exemption of $20,000 of assessed value for homeowners age 70 or more.	
$4,800 (value of property not to exceed $15,000)	Elderly homeowners are exempt from property tax up to $75.	Reduction in tax bill ($.72)
$10,000 implicit	Relief based on amount by which property tax (or rent constituting property tax) exceeds 6 percent of household income for that year on the amount of such income between zero and $3,000 plus 7% on that amount in excess of $3,000. Relief limit is $500 less 5% of household income. (25% of rent = tax equivalent).	State rebate ($2.58)
None	Maximum reduction of $1,500 from assessed value.	Reduction in tax bill (na)
$6,000 (realty value not in excess of $6,500)	Exemption of $1,000 assessed value.	Reduction in tax bill ($1.59)
$5,000	Relief ranges from 75% of property tax for incomes below $500 to 10% for incomes above $4,000. Limitation on amount of property tax liability considered for relief is $500. (20% of rent = tax equivalent, [15% if furnished or utilities provided]).	
	[In addition, all homeowners, regardless of age or income, receive a general credit financed by the state.]	

State	Financed by	Date of adoption	Description of beneficiaries (estimated number of claimants)
Iowa	State (circuit breaker) [replaces 1967 state-financed program]	1973	Homeowners and renters 65 and over or totally disabled (na)
Kansas	State (circuit breaker)	1970 1973 rev.	Homeowners 60 and over (na)
Kentucky	Localities (mandated)	1971	Homeowners 65 and over (125,000)
Louisiana	Homestead exemption of $2,000 of assessed value for all homeowners is mandated by state. No reimbursement to local government.		
Maine	State (circuit breaker)	1971 1973 rev.	Homeowners and renters 62 and older (16,000)
Maryland	Localities (mandated)	1967 1969 rev.	Homeowners 65 and over (61,000)
	Localities (mandated)	1968 1972 rev.	Homeowners 65 and over (females 62 and over in Cecil Co.)
Massachusetts	Localities (mandated)	1963 1971 rev.	Homeowners 70 and over (74,000)
Michigan	State (circuit breaker) [replaces 1965 state-financed program]	1973	All homeowners and renters

Income ceiling	Tax relief formula (or general remarks)	Form of relief (estimated per capita cost)
$6,000	Relief ranges from 95% of property tax for incomes below $1,000 to 25% for incomes above $5,000. Not more than $600 considered for relief. (20% of rent = tax equivalent). [In addition, all homeowners, regardless of age or income, receive a general credit financed by the state.]	State rebate
$8,192	Taxes in excess of various percentages of income, ranging from zero percent for incomes below $3,000 to 13% for incomes above $8,000. Limitation on amount of property tax liability considered for relief is $400.	State rebate ($2.88)
None	Exemption of $6,500 assessed value, except for assessment of special benefits.	Reduction in tax bill ($3.12)
$4,500 single $5,000 married (in addition net assets must not exceed $20,000)	Taxes in excess of various percentages of income, ranging from 2% for income below $1,000 to 16% for incomes above $4,000. (20% of rent = tax equivalent) (at least 35% of household income must be attributable to claimant).	State rebate only ($1.60)
$5,000	Credit of 50% of assessed value or $4,000, whichever is less, multiplied by the local property tax rate.	Reduction in tax bill ($1.81)
Varies by county	Relief varies from an increase in the credit provided by the state mandated law to a lessening or modification of conditions of eligibility for such credit.	Reduction in tax bill ($5.18)
$6,000 single $7,000 married (maximum estate: $40,000 single $45,000 married)	Exemption of $4,000 assessed value or the sum of $350, whichever would result in an abatement of the greater amount of taxes due.	Reduction in tax bill ($5.18)
None	Excess taxes are taxes above 3.5% of income [various lower percentages for elderly with incomes below $6,000]. Credit = 60% of excess taxes [100% for all elderly]. Maximum relief is $500. [17% of rent = property tax equivalent].	State income tax credit or rebate ($27.53)

State	Financed by	Date of adoption	Description of beneficiaries (estimated number of claimants)
Minnesota	State (circuit breaker)	1967 1973 rev.	Homeowners and renters 65 and over (95,000)
Mississippi	State finances a partial homestead exemption of $5,000 for all homeowners with a reimbursement to local governments.		
Missouri	State (circuit breaker)	1973	Homeowners and renters 65 and over
Montana	Localities (mandated)	1969 1971 rev.	Retired homeowners (na)
Nebraska	State	1972 1973 rev.	Homeowners 65 and over (60,000)
Nevada	State (circuit breaker)	1973	Homeowners and renters, 62 and over (13,000)
New Hampshire	Localities (optional)	1969	Homeowners 70 and over (9,300)
New Jersey	State 50% Localities 50% (mandated)	1953 1972 rev.	Homeowners 65 and over (163,000)
New Mexico	State (circuit breaker)	1972 1973 rev.	All persons (70,000)
New York	Localities (optional)	1972	Renters in rent-controlled housing, 62 and over (na)
	Localities (optional)	1966 1972 rev.	Homeowners 65 and over (82,000)
North Carolina	Localities (mandated)	1971 1973 rev.	Homeowners 65 and over (retired) (19,000)

Income ceiling	*Tax relief formula (or general remarks)*	*Form of relief (estimated per capita cost)*
$6,000	A percentage of tax is given back as a credit, percentage declines as income increases. Not more than $800 tax considered. (20% of rent = tax equivalent) [In addition, all homeowners, regardless of age or income, receive a general credit financed by the state.]	State income tax credit or rebate ($2.38)
$7,500	Tax exceeding various percentages of income is remitted; percentages range from 3% for incomes below $3,000 to 4% for incomes above $4,500. Not more than $400 tax considered for relief. (18% of rent = tax equivalent).	State income tax credit or rebate
$4,000 single $5,200 married	50% reduction.	Reduction of tax bill ($1.39)
$2,800 single $3,550 married $4,300 married and spouse over 65	Exemption of 90% of first $7,500 of assessed value for 1973 ($15,000 for 1974 and thereafter.) Maximum $125 in 1973 ($250 in 1974). (In addition to the state-financed general homestead exemption for all homeowners—amount of exemption depends on value of homestead.)	Reduction of tax bill (na)
$5,000	Property tax in excess of 7% is refunded (15% of rent = property tax equivalent). Maximum relief is $350.	State rebate ($1.42)
$4,000 single $5,000 married	Equalized valuation reduced by $5,000 times the local assessment ratio.	Reduction of tax bill ($1.99)
$5,000 (excluding Social Security)	Reduction of tax bill by $160, but not more than amount of tax.	Reduction of tax bill (one-half reimbursed by state) ($3.50)
$6,000	Person receives credit based on all state-local taxes which he is presumed to have paid. Credit varies depending on income and number of personal exemptions, ranges up to $133.	State income tax credit or rebate ($1.88)
$3,000 (can be raised to $5,000 by locality)	Not to exceed amount by which maximum rent exceeds one-third of combined household income.	Reduction of maximum rent (na)
$3,000 (can be raised to $6,000 by locality)	Assessed valuation reduced by 50%.	Reduction of tax bill ($1.14)
$5,000	Assessed valuation reduced by $5,000.	Reduction of tax bill ($.16)

State	Financed by	Date of adoption	Description of beneficiaries (estimated number of claimants)
North Dakota	Localities (mandated)	1969 1973	Homeowners 65 and over (5,000)
	State (circuit breaker)	1973	Renters 65 and over
Ohio	State (circuit breaker)	1971 1973 rev.	Homeowners 65 and over (na)
Oklahoma	Homestead exemption of $1,000 of assessed value for all homeowners is mandated by state. No reimbursement to local government.		
Oregon	State (circuit breaker)	1971 1973 rev.	All homeowners and renters (100,000)
Pennsylvania	State (circuit breaker)	1971 1973 rev.	Homeowners and renters 65 and over, and totally disabled
Rhode Island	Localities (optional)	1960 1973 rev.	Homeowners 65 and over (19,000)
South Carolina	State	1971 1973 rev.	Homeowners 65 and over (78,000)
South Dakota	Localities (mandated)	1972	Homeowners 65 and over (na)
Tennessee	State	1972	Homeowners 65 and over (81,000)
Texas	Localities (optional)	1972	Homeowners 65 and over (na)
Utah	Localities (optional)	1967 1973 rev.	Indigent homeowners (presumed to be 65 and over) (na)
Vermont	State (circuit breaker)	1969 1973 rev.	All homeowners and renters (60,000)
Virginia	Localities (optional)	1971 1973 rev.	Homeowners 65 and over

Income ceiling	Tax relief formula (or general remarks)	Form of relief (estimated per capita cost)
$3,500	Assessed valuation reduced by $1,000.	Reduction in tax bill ($.47)
$3,500	Property tax in excess of 5% of income is re-funded. (20% of rent = tax equivalent). Maximum relief is $350.	State rebate
$10,000	Benefits range from reduction of 70% or $5,000 assessed value (whichever is less) for incomes below $2,000 to 40% or $2,000 for incomes above $6,000.	Reduction of tax bill ($2.78)
$15,000	Refund of all property taxes, up to various maximums that depend on income ($490 for incomes below $500) (17% of rent = tax equivalent).	State rebate
$7,500	100% of tax for income less than $3,000 (max. rebate $200). 10% of tax for income greater than $7,000. (20% of rent = tax equivalent.)	State rebate
$4,000 ($5,000 in one locality)	Various formulas; most reduce assessed valuation by $1,000. [Also a tax freeze.]	Reduction in tax bill ($1.02)
None	Not related to income. Assessed valuation reduced by $10,000.	Reduction in tax bill ($1.31)
$4,000 married $2,400 single	Assessed valuation reduced by $1,000.	Reduction in tax bill ($5.15)
$4,800	Equivalent to reduction of assessment by $5,000.	State rebate to taxpayer ($.74)
None	Assessment reduced by $3,000.	Reduction in tax bill ($4.29)
$2,500 single $3,000 married	Taxes may be reduced by $100 or 50%, whichever is less.	Reduction in tax bill ($.16)
None	Refund of Taxes Exceeding Following Percent of Income Income Percentage 0–$3,999 4% $4,000–$7,999 4.5% $8,000–11,999 5.0% $12,000–15,999 5.5% $16,000– 6.0% Maximum relief is $500. (20% of rent = tax equivalent)	State rebate (or income tax credit for elderly) ($23.38)
$7,500 ($20,000 asset test)	At discretion of locality.	Reduction in tax bill

State	Financed by	Date of adoption	Description of beneficiaries (estimated number of claimants)
Washington	Localities (mandated)	1971	Homeowners 62 and over or disabled (72,000)
West Virginia	State (circuit breaker)	1972	Homeowners and renters 65 and over (na)
	Localities (mandated)	1973	Homeowners, 65 and over
Wisconsin	State (circuit breaker)	1964 1973 rev.	All homeowners and renters (79,000)
Wyoming	State	1973	Homeowners 65 and over (8,000)

Income ceiling	Tax relief formula (or general remarks)	Form of relief (estimated per capita cost)
$6,000	Income Percentage of excess levies abated 0–$4,000 100% $4,000–$6,000 50% (minimum relief of $50 for income below $4,000)	Reduction in tax bill ($1.81)
$5,000	Taxes exceeding a given percent of income is remitted. These percents range from .5% to 4.5%. Not more than $125 tax considered for relief. (12% of rent = tax equivalent.)	State rebate ($.84)
None	Exemption of $5,000 assessed value.	Reduction of tax bill
$7,000	Excess taxes are taxes above 14.3% of income exceeding $3,500. Credit = 80% of excess taxes. Not more than $500 tax considered for relief. (25% of rent = tax equivalent.) [In addition, all homeowners, regardless of age or income, receive a general credit financed by the state.]	State income tax credit or rebate
$2,000 single $2,500 married	Exemption of $1,000 assessed value.	Reduction in tax bill ($1.16)

na—Data not available.

Circuit breaker—A state-financed program of property tax relief in which the amount of tax relief phases out as household income rises. "Rev." indicates the year of the most recent liberalization of the above property tax relief program.

SOURCE: Advisory Commission on Intergovernmental Relations staff compilation based on Commerce Clearing House, *State Tax Reporter;* State of Washington, Department of Revenue, *Property Tax Relief in Washington,* October 1972; and telephone and letter survey of the various states.

State	Date of adoption	Description of beneficiaries (number of beneficiaries)	Income ceiling
Arizona[a]	1973	Homeowners and renters 65 and over (na)	$3,500 single, $5,000 married (assessed value of all property not to exceed $5,000)
Arkansas[b]	1973	Homeowners 65 and over (2,798)	$5,500
California[c]	1967 1973 rev.	Homeowners 62 and over (302,000)	$10,000 net $20,000 gross
Colorado	1971 1973 rev. 1974 rev.	Homeowners and renters 65 and over or disabled (27,251)	$5,900 single, $6,900 married (net worth less than $30,000— home, furniture, clothing, and car excluded)
Connecticut[d]	1973 1974 rev.	Homeowners and renters 65 and over (19,533)	$6,000
District of Columbia[e]	1974	Homeowners and renters (na)	$7,000

Supplement J

Key Features of State Circuit-Breaker Property Tax Relief Programs: 1974

Description of program	Form of relief	Average benefit (per capita cost) [total cost ($1,000)]
A percentage of tax is returned as a credit; credit declines as income rises. Only taxes on first $2,000 of assessed value are considered (25% of rent equals tax equivalent, up to $225).	State income tax credit or rebate	na (na) [na]
Taxes exceeding various percentages of income are remitted; percentages range from 1% on income below $1,500 to 5% on incomes above $4,500.	State income tax credit or rebate	$59.34 (0.08) [166]
Relief ranges from 96% of tax payment on first $7,500 of value if net household income is less than $1,400 to 4% of tax payment if net household income is $10,000 (additionally there is a state-financed homestead exemption of $1,750 for all homeowners).	State rebate	$201.98 (2.96) [61,000]
Relief cannot exceed $400 and is equal to $400 reduced by 10% of income over $2,000 for individuals and 10% of income over $3,000 for married couples (20% of rent equals tax equivalent).	State income tax credit or rebate	$86.41 (0.96) [2,355]
Taxes exceeding 5% of income. Maximum refund ranges up to $400 for incomes below $3,000 (20% of rent equals tax equivalent).	Reduction in tax bill	$317.05 (2.10) [6,193]
Relief takes the form of a variable credit ranging from 80% of tax in excess of 2% of income for incomes less than $3,000 to 60% of tax in excess of 4% of income for incomes over $5,000. Maximum tax of $400 used in figuring credit (15% of rent equals tax equivalent).	Income tax credit	na (na) [na]

163

State	Date of adoption	Description of beneficiaries (number of beneficiaries)	Income ceiling
Idaho	1974	Homeowners age 65 and over (15,924)	$5,000
Illinois[f]	1972 1974 rev.	Homeowners and renters 65 and over or disabled (144,647)	$10,000 implicit in formula, although not stated
Indiana	1973	Homeowners and renters 65 and over, disabled (44,000)	$5,000
Iowa	1973	Homeowners and renters 65 and over or totally disabled (15,924)	$6,000
Kansas	1970 1973 rev.	Homeowners 60 and over, or disabled (31,307)	$8,150
Maine	1971 1973 rev. 1974 rev.	Homeowners and renters 62 and over (13,468)	$4,500 single; $5,000 married.
Maryland[g]	1974	All homeowners and renters (na)	None
Michigan[h]	1973	All homeowners and renters (1,011,709)	None

Description of program	Form of relief	Average benefit (per capita cost) [total cost ($1,000)]
Relief ranges from lesser of $200 or actual taxes for those with incomes $3,000 or less to lesser of $100 or taxes for those with incomes of $5,000.	Reduction of tax bill	$117.49 (2.42) [1,871]
Relief based on amount by which property tax (or rent equivalent) exceeds 6% of first $3,000 of household income plus 7% of income in excess of $3,000. Relief limit is $500 less 5% of household income (25% of rent equals tax equivalent).	State rebate	$151.74 (1.95) [21,950]
Relief ranges from 75% of property tax for incomes below $500 to 10% for incomes above $4,000. Relief limit is $500 (20% of rent equals tax equivalent [15% if furnished or utilities provided]).	Income tax credit or rebate	$40.90 (0.33) [1,800]
Relief ranges from 95% of property tax for incomes below $1,000 to 25% for incomes above $5,000. Property taxes are limited to $600 for calculating relief (20% of rent equals tax equivalent).	State rebate	$117.49 (2.42) [2,540]
Taxes in excess of various percentages of income, ranging from 0% for incomes below $3,000 to 13% for incomes above $8,000. Property taxes are limited to $400 for calculating relief.	State rebate	$100.58 (1.38) [3,149]
Relief equal to amount of tax less 21% of household income in excess of $3,000. Relief cannot exceed $400 (25% of rent equals tax equivalent).	State rebate	$146.56 (1.92) [1,974]
Relief, not to exceed $750, equals property tax exceeding sum of graduated schedule of percentages of income ranging from 3% of first $3,000 of household income to 9% of income over $15,000 (up to 12% of rent equals tax equivalent).	Credit against property tax bill (cash payment to renters)	na (na) [na]
Credit equals 60% of property taxes in excess of 3.5% of income (100% of a lower percentage of income for elderly). Maximum relief is $500 (17% of rent equals tax equivalent).	State income tax credit or rebate	$148.58 (16.62) [150,300]

State	Date of adoption	Description of beneficiaries (number of beneficiaries)	Income ceiling
Minnesota[i]	1967 1973 rev.	Homeowners and renters 65 and over or disabled (110,000)	$6,000
Missouri	1973	Homeowners and renters 65 and over (58,031)	$7,500
Nevada	1973	Homeowners and renters 65 and over (1,994)	$5,000[i]
North Dakota[j]	1973	Renters 65 and over (5,052)	$3,500
Ohio	1971 1973 rev.	Homeowners 65 and over (264,300)	$10,000
Oklahoma[k]	1974	Homeowners age 65 and over or disabled (na)	$6,000
Oregon	1971 1973 rev.	All homeowners and renters (509,000)	$15,000
Pennsylvania	1971 1973 rev.	Homeowners and renters 65 and over or disabled (410,000)	$7,500
Vermont	1969 1973 rev.	All homeowners and renters (26,400)	None
West Virginia	1972	Homeowners and renters age 65 and over (8,529)	$5,000

Description of program	Form of relief	Average benefit (per capita cost) [total cost ($1,000)]
A percentage of tax is returned as a credit; percentage declines as income increases. No more than $800 tax considered (20% of rent equals tax equivalent).	State income tax credit or rebate	$91.00 (2.56) [10,010]
Tax exceeding various percentages of income is remitted; percentages range from 3% for incomes below $3,000 to 4% for incomes above $4,500. Not more than $400 tax considered for relief (18% of rent equals tax equivalent).	State income tax credit or rebate	$81.14 (0.98) [4,709]
Property tax in excess of 7% of income is refunded. Maximum relief is $300 (15% of rent equals tax equivalent).[1]	State rebate	$40.12 (0.14) [80]
Property tax in excess of 5% of income is refunded. Maximum relief is $100 (20% of rent equals tax equivalent).	State rebate	$70.00 (0.55) [35]
Benefits range from reduction of 70% or $5,000 assessed value (whichever is less) for incomes below $2,000 to 40% or $2,000 for incomes above $6,000.	Reduction of tax bill	$124.86 (3.20) [33,000]
Relief equal to property taxes due in excess of 1% of household income, not to exceed $200.	Refundable income tax credit	na (na) [na]
Refund of all property taxes up to various maximums that depend on income ($490 for incomes below $500) (17% of rent equals tax equivalent).	Refundable income tax credit	$138.95 (31.78) [70,730]
Relief ranges from 100% of tax for incomes less than $3,000 (maximum relief $200) to 10% of tax for incomes greater than $7,000 (20% of rent equals equivalent).	State rebate	$136.82 (4.71) [56,100]
Refund of taxes exceeding variable percent of income ranging from 4% for incomes less than $4,000 to 6% for incomes over $16,000. Maximum relief is $500 (20% of rent equals tax equivalent).	State rebate (or income tax credit for elderly)	$179.20 (10.19) [4,731]
Taxes exceeding a given percentage of income are remitted. These percents range from 0.5% to 4.5% (12% of rent equals tax equivalent; not more than $125 considered for relief).	State rebate	$19.46 (0.09) [166]

State	Date of adoption	Description of beneficiaries (number of beneficiaries)	Income ceiling
Wisconsin	1964 1973 rev.	All homeowners and renters (189,521)	$7,000

[a] Program took effect calendar-year 1974. First claims were to be filed January 1975.

[b] Relief currently takes the form of cash refunds as those having an income tax liability fail to qualify for property tax rebate.

[c] California also has a program to provide property tax relief to all renters, regardless of income or age. California expects an increase of 40,000–50,000 participants in FY 1975 as welfare recipients become eligible for the program for the first time.

[d] Homeowners in Connecticut now have the option of circuit-breaker relief or a property tax freeze. Both programs reduce tax bill.

[e] Took effect January 1, 1975.

[f] Relief formula changed January 1, 1975. New formula grants relief for property tax in excess of 4% of *all* income. Same limits will apply.

Description of program	Form of relief	*Average benefit (per capita cost)* [*total cost ($1,000)*]
Excess taxes are taxes above 14.3% of income exceeding $3,500. Tax credit equals 80% of excess taxes. Not more than $500 tax considered for relief (25% of rent equals tax equivalent).	State income tax credit or rebate	$186.84 (7.75) [35,411]

g The Maryland program was not funded in 1974, when it was adopted, and takes effect in 1975; if funded.

h In 1974 Michigan extended circuit-breaker coverage to farmers as well as owners of residential property. Farmers must agree to restrict land use to obtain relief, however.

i Homeowners 65 and over also participate in a property tax freeze program wherein the state will refund property tax increases.

j North Dakota has a separate program which lowers the assessed value of low-income elderly homeowners by as much as $1,000.

k The Oklahoma program took effect January 1, 1975, and grants relief for taxes paid in 1974.

l In addition to the income ceiling, this is a property ownership test; claimant must not own real estate (other then the home) assessed at more than $30,000.

SOURCE: Advisory Commission of Intergovernmental Relations staff compilation from questionnaire responses and Commerce Clearing House data.

Exemption of Properties from Taxation

In late 1972, a Senate subcommittee sent a questionnaire to all 50 states and the District of Columbia. Among the questions:

> (a) Does your State exempt any real property from ad valorem taxation?
> (b) If so, please give details of the kinds of property exempted.

Responses were received from all but one (Connecticut).

ALABAMA

Persons and classes of property are exempted from taxation on the basis of the attached material. Title 51, chapter 2, Code of Alabama.

ALASKA

Yes. Required exemptions are itemized in AS 29.53.020 as follows:
1. Government owned property.
2. Property used exclusively for nonprofit religious, charitable, cemetery, hospital or educational purposes.
3. Organizations composed of veterans with a minimum of 90-days active service in the armed forces of the United States.
4. The real property of qualifying senior citizens.
5. An option to municipalities is provided for exemption of private property used exclusively for community purposes and for historic sites.

Optional exemptions and exclusions are itemized in **AS** 29.53.025 as follows:

(a) Municipalities may exclude or exempt or partially exempt residential property from taxation by ordinance ratified by the voters at a regular or special election.

(b) Municipalities may by ordinance (1) classify boats and vessels for purposes of taxation and may establish the assessed valuation of boats and vessels on the basis of their registered or certified net tonnage; a tax based upon a tonnage valuation shall not exceed $5 a year for a boat or vessel of less than 5 net tons and shall not exceed $15 a year for a boat or vessel of more than 5 net tons; (2) classify and exempt from taxation—

(A) the household furniture over $500 in value and the effects of the head of a family or a householder; and

(B) the property of an organization not organized for business or profit making purposes and used exclusively for community purposes, provided that income derived from rental of such property does not exceed the actual cost to the owner of the use by the renter; and

(C) historic sites, buildings and monuments

(c) The provisions of (a) of this section notwithstanding, (1) a home rule of first- or second-class borough may, by ordinance adopted without weighted voting, adjust its property tax structure of a city within it, including but not limited to, excluding personal property from taxation, establishing exemption, and extending the redemption period; (2) a home rule or first class city shall have the same power to grant exemptions or exclude property from borough taxes that it has as to city taxes, provided that the exemptions or exclusions have been adopted as to city taxes and further provided that the city appropriate to the borough sufficient money to equal revenues lost by the borough because of the exemptions or exclusions, the amount to be determined annually by the assembly without weighted voting.

(d) Exemptions or exclusions from property tax which have been granted by home rule municipalities in addition to exemptions authorized or required by law, and which are in effect on September 10, 1972, and not later withdrawn are not affected by this Act.

ARIZONA

The State exempts the real property owned by religious and charitable institutions and used exclusively for worship purposes from ad valorem taxation. Also, a certain amount of property owned by widows and veterans is exempt, provided proper application is made and the applicant qualifies under some rigid statutory requirements.

ARKANSAS

Again, quoting from Arkansas' constitution (art. 16, sec. 5):

TAXATION EXEMPTIONS—GENERAL

The following property shall be exempt from taxation: Public property used exclusively for public purposes; churches used as such; cemeteries used exclusively as such; school buildings and apparatus; libraries and grounds used exclusively for school purposes, and buildings and grounds and materials used exclusively for public charity.

OTHER EXEMPTIONS FORBIDDEN

All laws exempting property from taxation other than as provided in this constitution shall be void.

CALIFORNIA

California exempts the following kinds of property from taxation:
  a. Public property,
  b. College property,
  c. Property used for religious, hospital, or charitable purposes (includes churches and orphanages), and
  d. Property of veterans.

COLORADO

Section 4 of the Colorado's Enabling Act provides "that no taxes shall be imposed by the State on lands or property therein belonging to, or which may hereafter be purchased by the United States."

Article X, section 4, of Colorado's constitution and 1963 CRS, 137–2–1, as amended, exempts the property, real and personal of the State, counties, cities, towns, and other municipalities, corporations, and public libraries.

1963 CRS, 139–31–22–6, exempts the real property of nonprofit cemetery companies.

1963 CRS, 137–61–1 and 2, exempts the property leased by municipal corporations provided the property is leased for long-term rental and is used for proprietary purposes.

1963 CRS, 69-3-27, exempts the property owned by a housing authority.

1963 CRS, 139–62–10, exempts all property acquired by an urban renewal authority.

1963 CRS 137–2–1 (6), (7), and (8) as amended, exempts the property, real and personal, that is owned and used solely and exclusively for religious worship; that is owned and used exclusively for schools; and that which is owned and used exclusively for strictly charitable purposes. In determining that property which is used solely and exclusively for strictly charitable purposes, the Colorado Supreme Court has followed Grey's rule which, in turn, has incorporated much of the statute of Elizabeth.

In addition, under property owned and used solely and exclusively for strictly charitable purposes, Colorado's Legislature has granted tax exemption to those portions of senior citizens homes wherein the occupants are 62 years of age or over and whose income and assets are within 150 percent of the limits prescribed for low-rent public housing pursuant to chapter 8, title 42, United States Code.

1963 CRS 137–2–2, exempts the first $6,000 of assessed value of any parcel of improved real property owned by a church or synagogue that is used solely and exclusively as the residence or dwelling of a minister, preacher, priest, or rabbi.

1963 CRS 137–3–17 as amended gives the property tax administrator authority to determine the taxable status of that property which is owned and used solely and exclusively for religious worship, that is owned and used solely and exclusively for schools, and that which is owned and used exclusively for strictly charitable purposes.

DELAWARE

Prior to fiscal year 1972, the State General Assembly was responsible for granting tax exemption to property owners. After fiscal year 1972 the counties and municipalities were given the right to grant these exemptions. Exemptions are usually given to elderly, low-income families.

DISTRICT OF COLUMBIA

Real property exempted from ad valorem taxation in the District of Columbia includes that owned by the U.S. Government, foreign governments (when used for legation purposes) and the District of Columbia government. Property is also exempted if used for charitable, educational or religious purposes. The list of property uses which qualify a property for exemption (District of Columbia Code of 47-801a) includes: (1) public art galleries; (2) public libraries; (3) hospitals; (4) schools, colleges, universities; (5) properties housing various scientific research activities; (6) cemeteries; (7) churches and other properties used for religious properties; (8) pastorial and episcopal residences. There are specific characteristics of ownership (not for private gain) and terms of use as prerequisites to the general exemption under these general exemption clauses.

Additionally, many properties are specifically exempted by provisions of the District of Columbia Code. It appears that some of these properties would be exempted, as well, under the general provision.

FLORIDA

Exemptions of real property from ad valorem taxation: A homestead exemption of $5,000 is granted to property owners. The exemption is increased to $10,000 from taxes levied by school boards for current school operating expenses if the homesteader is 65 and has been a permanent Florida resident for 5 prior years.

Homestead property owned by totally and permanently disabled veterans is totally exempt. The exemption carries over to the widow should her husband predecease her. The same exception is granted to disabled veterans confined to wheelchairs. Homestead property of quadriplegics is totally exempt.

Exemptions are granted for property used for exempt purposes; that is, charitable, religious, educational, scientific.

Property owned by any widow, blind person, or totally and permanently disabled person receives a $500 exemption.

GEORGIA

The following property is exempt from taxation:
   (a) places of religious worship or burial; single family residential property owned by religious institutions from which no income is derived
   (b) public property
   (c) nonprofit hospitals
   (d) nonprofit educational institutions
   (e) institutions of purely public property. . . .

In addition, Georgia has a $2,000 homestead regular exemption, and a $4,000 homestead exemption for certain elderly persons. Authorization has been provided for total school tax exemption on the homestead of certain elderly persons.

HAWAII

Yes. [Reference to] "Tax Exemption and Tax Concession Report for the State of Hawaii (1970)" . . . Briefly, there are real property exemptions for the homeowner, the disabled, including veterans, leprosy, charitable, nonprofit organizations such as churches, educational institutions, hospitals, union, et cetera, public utilities. Federal land, State land, and county land, low- and moderate-income housing.

IDAHO

Yes. Homes of widows and elderly to limited degree; nonprofit corporations, if not used in profit generation; churches, schools, United States, and other government property.

ILLINOIS

Real property exemptions are set forth in . . . Chapter 120, section 500.

INDIANA

The Indiana constitution enables the general assembly to exempt by law real property used for municipal, educational, literary, scientific, religious or charitable purposes. Generally, exemptions in whole or part from ad valorem taxation are granted for real property owned and/or used by: national, State, and municipal governments; nonprofit educational, literary, scientific, religious and charitable purposes; cemeteries; certain historical sites; nonprofit rural water corporations; persons owning mortgaged property, those age 65 and over, the blind, disabled veterans, and widows of veterans; rehabilitated property, public airports; certain housing authorities, and navigation companies.

IOWA

(a) Yes.

(b) Real property of the Federal and State governments. Also, real property of a county, city, town, township, school corporation, levee district, drainage district, or military company of the State of Iowa, when devoted to public use and not held for pecuniary profit, cemeteries, fire equipment; property of associations of war veterans; libraries and art galleries; property of religious, charitable, benevolent, literary, agricultural, and scientific institutions and societies when used for their appropriate objects and not leased or otherwise held with a view to pecuniary profit; property held in the endowment fund of an educational institution; certain agricultural produce; family or household equipment; public airports. Property to a certain valuation of war veterans. Credits against computed property tax are allowed owners of homesteads who qualify for same, and credits against tax are allowed owners of intangible personal property who qualify for same (credit not to exceed $2,700 of assessed valuation).

KANSAS

Kansas exempts the following real property from ad valorem taxation:
  (a) Buildings and grounds used exclusively for public worship or public education if not leased or otherwise used for profit.
  (b) Cemetery lots and tracts for grave sites of individual owners.
  (c) Real property actually used exclusively for literary, educational, scientific, religious, benevolent, or charitable purposes, as long as it is in no way used as an investment.

(d) Property belonging exclusively to the United States.

(e) Property used exclusively by the State of Kansas or any municipality or political subdivision of the State.

(f) Under certain conditions, property constructed or purchased by means of industrial revenue bonds or improvement district bonds, depending on specific statutory provisions.

(g) Property used exclusively by rural or township water districts.

(h) Property used exclusively in connection with the function of fire extinguishment.

KENTUCKY

See . . . Section 170, State Constitution.

LOUISIANA

The State has an exemption for industrial property (manufacturing) for a period of 10 years.

MAINE

There are exemptions applicable to certain governmental and institutional real estate, and real estate of certain veterans and others. There is no exception for real estate apart from ownership and use.

MARYLAND

Approximately 25 percent of the total real property in Maryland is exempt from taxation. These exemptions are generally to property owned by all levels of government, religious organizations, nonprofit educational charitable institutions, et cetera.

MASSACHUSETTS

Property of United States, Massachusetts, used for military, water company, qualified urban redevelopment corporations, housing authorities, special authorities, hospital insurance corporations, property owned by charitable and religious institutions.

MICHIGAN

Property of the United States Government.

Property of the State government.

Lands owned by any county, township, city, village, or school district used for public purposes.

Library, benevolent, charitable, educational or scientific institutions, and memorial homes of world war veterans.

Charitable homes of fraternal or secret societies.

Up to 400 acres of land owned by a boy or girl scout organization.

Hospitals.

Houses of public worship and the parsonage.

Cemeteries.

Hardship cases, those deemed to be eligible for exemption by the board of review.

Landing areas of private airports when available to the public without charge. . . .

Veteran's Homestead Tax Exemption:

This program provides property tax relief for veterans and servicemen (or their widows). To be eligible individuals must have been Michigan residents for at least 6 months prior to entering the Armed Forces and have been a resident of Michigan for at least 5 years prior to application for exemption. Incomes shall not exceed $7,500 and State equalized valuation of owned property shall not exceed $10,000. The amount of exemption varies with the degree of disability incurred during military service from $2,500 State equalized valuation to $4,500 State equalized valuation. A veteran receiving Veterans' Administration disability compensation is not subject to the income limitation. In fiscal year 1972, 60,494 veterans or their widows availed themselves of this exemption for a cost of $10 million.

Senior Citizen's Homestead Tax Exemption:

To be eligible for property tax relief, a senior citizen must be over the age of 65, a Michigan citizen for 5 of the last 10 immediately preceding years, and the combined income of the owners and occupants of the homesteads must not exceed $6,000. Up to $2,500 of the State equalized valuation of the homestead is exempt from taxation. During fiscal year 1972, 213,841 citizens availed themselves of this exemption for a total cost of $25 million.

Homestead Exemption for the Blind:

The homestead of a blind person is exempt up to $3,500 of State equalized valuation. In fiscal year 1972, 5,400 people availed themselves of this exemption for a cost of $950,000.

Property Tax Credit:

In addition to the above, a credit against the State income tax liability is allowed for property taxes paid. Seventeen percent of rent is considered the property tax paid by renters. The credit cannot exceed the income tax liability. The credit is calculated according to the following schedule:

If property tax is:

Less than $100, the credit is   20 percent of the property tax.

Less than $150 but greater than $100, the credit is	$20 plus 10 percent of the excess over $100.
Less than $200 but greater than $150, the credit is	$25 plus 5 percent of the excess over $150.
Less than $10,000 but greater than $200, the credit is	$27.50 plus 5 percent of the excess over $200.

It is estimated that in fiscal year 1972, 2 million people claimed this credit for a cost of $95 million.

MINNESOTA

Railroad and telephone property are exempted from ad valorem taxation and pay a gross earning tax in lieu thereof. Property of taconite iron mining and taconite processing plants are exempt and pay a per ton production tax in lieu thereof. Property of religious institutions and schools are exempt. Public property is exempt.

MISSISSIPPI

(a) Homestead up to $5,000 including 160 acres.
(b) Industrial real [property] up to 10 years at discretion of local boards.

MISSOURI

Section 6, article 10 of the Constitution of Missouri exempts certain classifications of property from taxation.

MONTANA

Yes, . . . [see] Section 84–202, State code.

NEBRASKA

Nebraska exempts the property of the State and its governmental subdivisions. Property owned by and used exclusively for agricultural and horticultural societies and property owned and used exclusively for educational, religious, charitable or cemetery purposes when such property is not owned or used for financial gain or profit. Further, the value of a home substantially contributed by the Veteran's Administration in the United States for a paraplegic veteran or multiple amputee shall be exempt from taxation for the life of such veteran or until the death of his widow or her remarriage.

In addition, there is a homestead exemption provision.

NEVADA

(a) Yes.

(b) Statutory provisions . . . [in] NRS 361.050 to 361.153.

NEW HAMPSHIRE

New Hampshire exempts the real property owned by religious, educational, and charitable organizations from taxation. The real and personal property of the American Red Cross and veterans organizations are also exempted. . . .

The elderly exemption is limited to persons over 70 years of age, with income from all sources not to exceed $5,000, if married, or $4,000, if single, and assets of all kinds not to exceed $25,000. The maximum benefit granted to qualifying elderly persons is a $5,000 valuation exemption in towns assessing at full value. If a town is not assessing at full value, the exemption is that proportion of $5,000 that the level of assessment bears to 100 percent. Veterans are given a $50 tax credit generally; however, totally and permanently disabled veterans (service connected) receive a tax credit of $600. Legally blind persons receive a $1,000 valuation exemption.

NEW JERSEY

The following real property is exempt from ad valorem taxation:

(1) property of the State and its political subdivisions; property used for military purposes; property of veterans' organizations; residences of district supervisors of religious organizations (N.J.S.A. 54:4–3.3, 54:4–3.35, 54:4–3.5);

(2) buildings of colleges, schools, academies, seminaries; publicly owned historical societies; public libraries; humane societies; religious, charitable, and benevolent associations; hospitals, volunteer first-aid squads; nonprofit corporations which permit use of their buildings by charitable or religious organizations either for compensation or rent-free parsonages—not exceeding two—plus accessory buildings; property held by the State federation of district boards of education; all property owned and used by mentally retarded, or idiotic men, women, or children, provided that such

corporation conduct and maintain research or professional training facilities for the care and training of such retarded individuals; and land not exceeding 5 acres upon which such buildings are located; all buildings in New Jersey used exclusively by nonprofit educational television associations or corporations, and the land on which located, but not over 30 acres (N.J.S.A. 54:4–3.6, 54:4–3.6a);

(3) graveyards and vaults intended to hold bodies or ashes of the dead (N.J.S.A. 54:4–3.9);

(4) real property of any exempt fireman's association, relief association, and volunteer fire company incorporated under the laws of the State and which is used exclusively for the purpose of the corporation (N.J.S.A. 54:4–3.10);

(5) all offices, and franchises, and all property used for railroad or canal purposes by a railroad or canal company subject to a New Jersey franchise tax (N.J.S.A. 4–3.11);

(6) property of domestic public fire patrol or salvage corps associations or corporations used exclusively for the public purpose of saving life and property from destruction by fire (N.J.S.A. 54:4–3.13);

(7) real estate not exceeding 250 acres owned, and actually and exclusively used, by any domestic corporation to provide instruction in agricultural pursuits for veterans who have been permanently crippled while in active service in time of war (N.J.S.A. 54:4–3.15);

(8) turnpike roads used by the public toll-free (N.J.S.A. 54:4–3.18);

(9) property of the following associations: Y.M.C.A., Y.W.C.A., Y.M. and Y.W.C.A., Y.M.H.A., Y.W.H.A., or Y.M. and Y.W.H.A., Boy Scouts, Girl Scouts (N.J.S.A. 54:4–3.25);

(10) property of bona fide national war veterans' organizations existing and established on June 18, 1936 (N.J.S.A. 54:4–3.26);

(11) property of fraternal organizations or lodges organized or operated for charitable or educational purposes (Ch. 320, Laws 1971; N.J.S.A. 54:4-3.26);

(12) property of the Red Cross, and other national and international relief organizations (N.J.S.A. 54:4–3.27);

(13) in addition to other exemptions granted on his real or personal property, the dwelling house and lot of an honorably discharged veteran having a service-connected disability from paraplegia, sarcoidosis, osteochondritis resulting in permanent loss of the use of both legs, or permanent paralysis of both legs and lower parts of the body, or from hemiplegia and permanent paralysis of one leg and one arm on either side of the body resulting from injury to the

spinal cord, total blindness, or from the amputation of both arms or both legs, or both hands or both feet, or the combination of a hand and a foot, or, if annual income of the taxpayer is not over $5,000, from other service-connected disability declared by the Veterans' Administration to be a total or 100 percent permanent disability; this exemption applies to the widow of a qualified veteran during her widowhood (Ch. 398, Laws 1971; N.J.S.A. 54:4–3.30);

(14) property of veterans, or their widows, in the amount of $50 from their final property tax bills; real property of resident senior citizens in the amount of $160 from their final tax bills, provided their annual income, including that of his or her spouse but not including social security benefits or benefits received under other Federal programs or State and local pension, disability or retirement programs, does not exceed $5,000 (S.B. 282, laws 1972; ch. 20, laws 1971; art. VIII, sec. 1, N.J. Const.; N.J.S.A. 54:5–8.11, 54:4–8.11a, 54:4–8.40, 54:4–8.41);

(15) Value of fallout shelters erected on residential property (N.J.S.A. 54:4–3.8);

(16) historic lands, buildings and contents (N.J.S.A. 54:4–3.52);

(17) senior citizens housing projects, and limited-dividend nonprofit housing projects, at the discretion of the municipality where located, are eligible for a 50-year exemption (N.J.S.A. 55:14I–5, 55:16–18);

(18) equipment used to abate or prevent air and water pollution, and the value of any improvement to realty in the form of any structure, machinery, equipment, device or facility necessary to the installation or maintenance of a potable water supply system or a water-carried sewerage disposal system (N.J.S.A. 54:4–3.56, 54:4–3.59, 54:4–3.60);

(19) main stem railroad property, tangible personal property of railroads, and facilities used in passenger service (N.J.S.A. 54:29A–7).

NEW MEXICO

Church, schools, charitable institutions. All government. . . . Veterans receive $2,000 off assessed value.

NEW YORK

New York State law provides an extensive series of partial and total exemptions from real property taxation for both publicly and privately owned real property. These statutes are contained primarily in the real property tax law (McKinney's Consolidated Laws of New York, annotated, vol. 49A).

In addition, a substantial series of partial exemptions relating to low- and middle-income housing projects is contained in various statutes such as the private housing finance law (McKinney's Consolidated Laws of New York, annotated, vol. 41) and the public housing law (McKinney's Consolidated Laws of New York, annotated, vol. 44A). These statutes provide a complex group of exemptions which vary in applicability, amount and duration.

NORTH CAROLINA

(a) Yes.
(b) Governmental property; property used for nonprofit educational, charitable, historical, cultural, patriotic and fraternal purposes, property used for religious worship, religious headquarters, and religious assemblies; nonprofit hospitals; and pollution abatement property.

NORTH DAKOTA

Real property belonging to municipalities, schools, nonprofit charitable institutions, churches (when used for religious purposes, hospitals (charitable), fairs, lodges, farm improvements, disabled veterans (partial) and blind (partial).

OHIO

For tax year 1971, the 88 county auditors, in compliance with the provisions of section 5713.07 and 5713.08 of the Ohio Revised Code, reported to the board of tax appeals a valuation of nearly $5 billion of exempted real property. The board annually publishes a compilation of these valuations by type, by county. The 1971 valuations of exempted real property are as follows:

	Valuation (millions)
United States of America	$641
State of Ohio	456
County	192
Township	42
Municipalities	697
Board of Education	1,232
Park district (public)	69
Colleges, academies (private)	327
Charitable institutions (private)	475
Churches, public worship	753
Graveyards monuments, cemeteries	74
Total	4,960

It should be noted that the valuation of tax-exempt property represents over 16 percent of the valuation of all real property in the State. Six counties have more than a third of their real property exempt from taxation; one small county with a Federal nuclear powerplant has 81 percent of its real property tax exempt.

OKLAHOMA

Exemptions of both real and personal property are controlled by article 10, sections 6 and 6A, and article 12–A of the Oklahoma constitution. Some exemptions apply only to personal property; others apply only to real property. Some apply to either real or personal property. Some exemptions apply to total value; others apply to specified limits of value. Some exemptions apply to all tax levies; others apply only to specified levies. A table has been prepared which outlines the basic exemption structure—a copy is attached. Examples of types of property exempted are given, but the examples given are only representative; they are not fully inclusive.

EXEMPTIONS FROM AD VALOREM TAXATION UNDER OKLAHOMA LAW AS OF JAN. 1, 1970

Exemption description	Constitutional authority	Statutory authority	Type of property exempted
1. Free public libraries	Art. 10, § 6	68 O.S. § 2405	Mixed
2. Free museums	Art. 10, § 6	68 O.S. § 2405	Mixed
3. Public cemeteries	Art. 10, § 6	68 O.S. § 2405	Mixed
4. Schools	Art. 10, § 6	68 O.S. § 2405	Mixed
5. Colleges	Art. 10, § 6	68 O.S. § 2405	Mixed
6. Property used for religious purposes.	Art. 10, § 6	68 O.S. § 2405	Mixed
7. Property used for charitable purposes.	Art. 10, § 6	68 O.S. § 2405	Mixed
8. Property of the United States.	Art. 10, § 6	68 O.S. § 2405	Mixed
9. Property of the State of Oklahoma.	Art. 10, § 6	68 O.S. § 2405	Mixed
10. Property of counties	Art. 10, § 6	68 O.S. § 2405	Mixed
11. Property of municipalities.	Art. 10, § 6	68 O.S. § 2405	Mixed

Maxi-mum assessed value exempted	Levies exempted	Examples
Total	All	City and/or county libraries.
Total	All	Public or private free museums.
Total	All	Any public cemetery.
Total	All	Public and private schools, including those organized for profit.
Total	All	Church sanctuaries.
Total	All	Charitable hospitals.
Total	All	FAA; Tinker AFB; etc.
Total	All	State capitol; court houses; city halls; housing author-
Total	All	ities; urban renewal au-
Total	All	thorities; public trusts; industrial development authorities.

Exemption description	Constitutional authority	Statutory authority	Type of property exempted
12. Household goods of the heads of families, tools, implements, and livestock employed in the support of the family.	Art. 10, § 6	68 O.S. § 2405	Personal
13. All growing crops	Art. 10, § 6	68 O.S. § 2405	Personal (except timber)
14. Family portraits	Art. 10, § 6	68 O.S. § 2405	Personal
15. Food, fuel, grain, and forage for the use of a family and its livestock, not to exceed 1 year's provisions.	Art. 10, § 6	68 O.S. § 2405	Personal
16. All game animals kept for propagation or exhibition purposes.	None	68 O.S. § 2405	Personal
17. Property of qualified veterans.	Art. 10, § 6	68 O.X. § 2045	Personal
18. Property of servicemen on active duty.	None	68 O.S. § 2405	Personal
19. Property of Whitaker Orphan Home	Art. 10, § 6	68 O.S. § 2505	Mixed
20. Property constituting a homestead.	Art. 12–A	68 O.S. § 2407	Real
21. Urban tracts larger than 5 acres.	Art. 10, § 6	11 O.S. §§ 481–482, + case law.	Real
22. All intangible personal property.	Art. 10, § 6A	None	Intangible personal
23. Goods, wares and merchandise in interstate movement ("Free port")	Art. 10, § 6A	68 O.S. § 2425	Personal
24. Property exempt under territorial law, not subsequently deprived of exemption by the Legislature.	Art. 10, § 6	None	Mixed

Maxi- mum assessed value exempted	Levies exempted	Examples
$100	All	Self-explanatory.
Total	All	Self-explanatory.
Total	All	Self-explanatory.
Total	All	Self-explanatory.
Total	All	Self-explanatory.
$200	All	Any tangible personalty.
$200	All	Any tangible personalty.
Total	All	Self-explanatory.
$1,000	All	Self-explanatory.
Total	Municipal	Such tracts used agriculturally, and not receiving ordinary municipal services.
Total	All	Cash, stocks, bonds, receivables, etc.
Total	All	Any merchandise entering Oklahoma, being held in the state not more than 9 months, for specified purposes, and then leaving Oklahoma.
Total	All	See No. 21.

Exemption description	Constitutional authority	Statutory authority	Type of property exempted
25. Property exempt by reason of treaty stipulations existing between the Indians and the U.S. Government, or by reason of Federal laws, during the force and effect of such treaties or federal laws.	Art. 10, § 6	68 O.S. § 2405	Mixed
26. Property of all fraternal and other orphan homes.	Art. 10, § 6	68 O.S. § 2405	Mixed
27. Property of a factory or public utility, as an inducement to its location, for a period not exceeding 5 years, when approved by a majority of the electors of the city or town, voting at an election called for that purpose.	Art. 10, § 6	11 O.S. § 6	Mixed

OREGON

[see] ORS, 308.345–395; 215.130–213; 321.605–680.

PENNSYLVANIA

Exemption from real property taxes is mandated by the constitution. Specific exemption is statutory. Current exemptions include churches and church grounds, nonprofit burial grounds, hospitals, universities, colleges, seminaries, academies, benevolent and charity institutions, fire and rescue stations, public schoolhouses, courthouses, jails, public parks, public property used for public purposes, playgrounds, public libraries, museums, concert halls, and art galleries.

RHODE ISLAND

There are two types of property tax exemptions in Rhode Island, statutory and personal. The exemptions include both personal and real property. Also, all classes of personal and real property are taxed at the same rate.

Maxi-mum assessed value exempted	Levies exempted	Examples
Total	All	Restricted Indian land.
Total	All	Self-explanatory.
Total	Municipal	Self-explanatory.

Therefore, it is difficult to separate out whether an exemption is actually for real or personal property or what classification of property is exempt. However, an analysis of exemptions would be an important indication of potential growth of the tax base for a small State like Rhode Island.

The following table lists the kinds and amounts of statutory exemptions for the 1972 tax roll:

Type:	*Assessed value of exemption*
Cemeteries	$12,666,222
Charities	13,141,752
Church	104,522,624
Ex-charter	30,594,465
Federal	341,788,158
Hospital	76,098,118
Libraries	8,379,449
Military	3,471,386
Municipal	195,405,224
School	311,718,571
State	201,926,011
Tax sales	451,145
Vote of city	9,810,279
Miscellaneous	82,320,587
Total assessed value	$1,392,293,991

There are several types of personal exemptions, which are listed below. To receive any of these exemptions the applicant must be a Rhode Island resident and must file an application with the local assessors office.

Type exemption:	Amount of exemption
Veterans (World War I, World War II, Merchant Marine in World War II, Korea, Viet Nam and others)	$1,000
Total service-connected disabled veteran	2,000
Total service-connected disabled veteran who lives in "specially adapted housing"	10,000
Unmarried widow of qualified veteran	1,000
Gold-Star parents (one only)	1,500
Totally blind residents	3,000
Fallout shelter, not exceeding	1,500
Persons 65 years of age and over (exemption, amount and conditions determined by city or town)	(1)
The estates, persons, and families of the president and professors for the time being of Brown University for each not more than $10,000 for each such officers, his estate, person, and family included	10,000

1 Usually $1,000 to $1,500, but sometimes a percentage of income.

The following table shows the amounts and type of personal exemptions for the 1972 tax roll.

Type exemption:	Assessed value of exemption
Blindness	$1,329,100
Elderly	20,147,400
Gold Star	740,210
Inability	3,319,080
Professor at Brown University	712,880
Reforestation	176
Veterans	85,479,907
Widows of veterans	938,605
Disabled veterans	164,730
Tax sale	41,500
Miscellaneous	817,085
Total assessed value of personal exemptions	$113,690,673

SOUTH CAROLINA

The State does exempt certain real property from the ad valorem tax. Article 10, section 4, of the South Carolina constitution exempts:

There shall be exempted from taxation all county, township, and municipal property used exclusively for public purposes and not for revenue, and the property of all schools, colleges, and institutions of learning, all charitable institutions in the nature of asylums for the infirm, deaf and dumb, blind, idiotic, and indigent persons, except where the profits of such institutions are applied to private uses; all public libraries, churches, parsonages, and burying grounds; but property of associations and societies, although connected with charitable objects, shall not be exempt from State, county, or municipal taxation: *Provided,* That as to real estate this exemption shall not extend beyond the buildings and premises actually occupied by such schools, colleges, institutions of learning, asylums, libraries, churches, parsonages, and burial grounds, although connected with charitable objects.

Provided, further, the general assembly may by act exempt from taxation household goods and furniture used in the home of the owner thereof.

SOUTH DAKOTA

Real property exemptions are given to all charitable, benevolent, and religious societies used for charitable, benevolent, and religious purposes. Of course, all property owned by all government entities are exempt.

TENNESSEE

(a) Yes.

(b) The property herein enumerated shall be exempt from taxation:

(1) All property of the United States, all property of the State of Tennessee, of any county, or of any incorporated city, town, or taxing district in the State that is used exclusively for public county or municipal purposes.

(2) The real estate owned by any religious, charitable, scientific, or educational institution occupied by such institution or its officers exclusively for carrying out thereupon one or more of the purposes for which said institution was created or exists.

(3) All cemeteries, places of burial used as such, and monuments of the dead.

(4) All roads, streets, alleys, and promenades where condemned, dedicated, or thrown open for public travel or use free of charge.

(5) All growing crops of whatever kind, the direct product of the soil of this State, in the hands of the producer or his immediate vendee, and articles manufactured from the produce of this State in the hands of the manufacturer.

(6) Personal property, not including that by way of income, of the value of $7,500 in the hands of each resident taxpayer; provided that any conveyance of personal property, including money, bank stock, notes, choses in action, accounts, or other evidence of indebtedness—in trust or otherwise—to any minor by the parent or parents thereof shall be presumed to have been made for the purpose of avoiding the payment of taxes thereon, if it appears that such conveyance affects enough personal property which, added to the amount, will exceed the aggregate, the amount heretofore set out as exempt from taxation, and it shall be the duty of the assessor to list all such property as the property of the person making such conveyance or creating such trust; provided, that the maker or makers of the trust instrument or conveyance or delivery of such property may appear before the county board of equalizers and by proof establish the bona fides of such trust or conveyance.

(7) All property protected by valid charter or contract exemption.

(8) Leasehold estates and improvements thereon, in the hands of the lessee, holding under incorporated institutions of learning in this State, when the rents therefor are used by said institutions purely for educational purposes, where the fee in the same is exempt from taxation to

said institutions of learning by charter granted by the State of Tennessee.

(9) Personal property which (a) is moving in interstate commerce through or over the territory of the State of Tennessee, or (b) was consigned to a warehouse within the State of Tenessee from outside the State of Tennessee, for storage, in transit, to a final destination (whether specified when transportation begins or afterwards) which is also outside the State of Tennessee, shall be deemed not to have acquired a situs in the State of Tennessee for purposes of ad valorem taxation.

(10) Personal property in the hands of the manufacturer, processer, or assembler, transported to a plant, warehouse or establishment within the State of Tennessee from outside the State, for storage, processing, assembly or repackaging, and held for eventual sale or other disposition, other than at retail, to a destination (whether specified when transportation begins or afterwards) which is outside this State, shall be deemed not to have acquired a situs within the State of Tennessee for purposes of ad valorem taxation.

In the event such personal property mentioned in this subdivision is held for sale or eventual disposition to destinations both within and without the State of Tennessee, then this exemption shall be applicable to that percentage of the value of such personal property, in the same proportion which sales or other dispositions to final destinations outside of the State of Tennessee during the preceding year, bears to the total sales of dispositions of such personal property by such manufacturer, processer, or assembler during such preceding year. This exemption is in addition to, and does not limit in any respect, all existing exemptions.

(11) The real estate owned or leased by an educational institution and used for dormitory purposes for its students, even though other student activities are conducted therein, and even though the student's spouse or children may reside therein.

(12) (a) All property of Tennessee not-for-profit general welfare corporations whose projects are financed by a loan made, insured, or guaranteed by a branch, department, or agency of the U.S. Government under §§ 202 or 236, either or both, of the national housing act, devoted to below-cost housing for elderly persons as defined by the national housing act, as amended, who have incomes not in excess of those established by the Department of Housing and Urban Development, shall be exempt from all ad valorem and personal taxes of any county, municipality, or metropolitan government so long as there is an unpaid balance outstanding on said loan and so long as the corporation remains not-for profit.

(13) Real property up to the value of $25,000 when such property is owned and is used exclusively by a disabled veteran as a home.

(14) All appliances, equipment, machinery, structures, or other such property or portion thereof used primarily and necessary for the control, reduction, or elimination of water or air pollution, provided that a certificate has been issued to the applicant by the Tennessee Department of Public Health.

TEXAS

[See] Vernon's Annotated Civil Statutes, article 7150, which enumerates the property exemptions in the State. . . . As you will notice, property is generally exempted on the basis of of ownership (e.g., churches, YMCA, Boy Scouts of America, and so forth) rather than particular use. The constitution also provides a $3,000 homestead exemption on residential property and an additional allowable homestead exemption for persons 65 years or older.

UTAH

Utah exempts properties used exclusively for religious and/or charitable purposes. This is a constitutional provision. Commercial enterprises owned by churches and other organizations which produce a profit are taxable. . . . Veterans or their surviving dependents may be allowed an exemption up to a maximum of $3,000 in assessed value, depending upon the extent of their disability as classified by the Government. Similar exemptions are allowed to the blind.

VERMONT

For all statutes concerning the exemption of real property from ad valorem taxation, please refer to . . . Ch. 125, secs. 3802-3, 3831-3844.

VIRGINIA

(a) See . . . Article X. sec. 6, State constitution.

(b) . . . Recent statutes authorize the governing body of any county, city, or town to levy a service charge on tax-exempt real estate. This would presumably authorize the local assessing officer to make a listing for such as required to be shown on the land book. Service charge charges extend to all tax-exempt real estate exclusive of churches and the residences of ministers and may not exceed 40 percent of the real estate rate.

WASHINGTON

Basically the real property that is exempted from the ad valorem tax is publicly owned property, schools, colleges, churches, certain cemeteries, certain nonsectarian character building or veteran and relief organizations, free public libraries, orphanages, institutions, non-profit nursing homes and hospitals.

WEST VIRGINIA

West Virginia exempts the following types of real property from ad valorem taxation:

(1) Government-owned property when used for public purposes.

(2) Property used for educational, literary, scientific, religious or charitable purposes and not leased or held up for profit. (The use of the property is controlling; use must be primarily and immediately for the exemptable purpose not secondary or remote. Pledging income from property for an exemptable purpose does not render the property exempt.)

(3) All cemeteries.

WISCONSIN

The general titles of real property exemptions are as follows: (From 1969 Statutes)

1. Property of the State
2. Municipal property
3. Colleges and Universities
3a. Building at Grand Army Home
4. Educational, Religious and Benevolent Institutions, Women's Clubs, Historical Societies, Fraternities, Libraries
4m. Nonprofit Hospitals
5. Agricultural Fairs
6. Fire Companies
7. Land of military organizations
8. Partial exemptions (special cases)
9. War veteran memorials and halls
10. YMCA and YWCA
10m. Lion Foundation Camps for Visually Handicapped Children
11. Bible Camps
12. Scouts and Boys Clubs of America
13. Cemeteries
14. Art Galleries
15. Community Centers (repealed in 1971)

16. Labor Temples
17. Farmers Temples
18. Property of Housing Authorities
19. Institutions for Dependent Children
20. Property held in trust in public interest (works of ancient man, etc.)
21. Treatment Plant and Pollution Abatement Equipment
22. Camps for the Handicapped (Wisconsin Easter Seal Society)
23. Nuclear attack shelters
24. Property in Conservation Area (Urban Renewal)
25. Nonprofit Medical Research Foundations
26. Property of Industrial Development Agencies while still in the hands of a county

The 1971 Legislature created chapter 215 which requires that each person who claims a real property tax exemption to file with the assessor a report prescribed by the Secretary of Revenue.

WYOMING

(a) Yes.
(b) Cities, Federal, State, airports, public libraries, churches, lots and buildings used exclusively for religious purposes, school districts except teacherages, county, fraternal and charitable properties. . . . Veteran exemption

Different Treatment of Farm and Open Space Land

By 1974, well over 30 states had modified their real property tax codes to give special treatment to certain eligible lands. Most commonly, the differential treatment is given to farmland; but some states also give special assessment treatment to forest land, open space land, recreation land, or lands of unusual historical, scenic, or ecological importance.

This summary of individual state laws was set out in a 1974 publication prepared by economists Thomas F. Hady and Ann Gordon Sibold and issued by the U.S. Department of Agriculture.

ALASKA

Alaska enacted a deferred tax law in 1967.

ELIGIBILITY

Farm use land ". . . means the use of land for raising, harvesting and marketing of crops, dairying and livestock management, . . . The owner must be actively engaged in farming the land and must derive at least one-fourth of his yearly gross income from the farm use land" [Alaska Statutes, § 29.53.035 (c)]. The owner must apply to the borough (county) tax assessor each year he wants to secure a farm use assessment [§ 29.53.035 (b)].

ASSESSMENT

"Farm use lands will be assessed on the basis of full and true value for farm use" [§ 29.53.035 (a)]. Where possible, the tax assessor will also record land value as if it were valued for nonfarm use.

199

CHANGE IN LAND USE

Should such farm use land subsequently be changed to another use, the owner will be liable for back taxes for the 2 preceding years. The amount due will be the difference between the tax paid based on a farm use assessment and the taxes which would have been paid based on a nonfarm use assessment [§ 29.53.035 (a)].

ARKANSAS

Arkansas enacted a preferential assessment law in 1969.

ELIGIBILITY

Farm, agricultural, and timber land actively employed in those respective uses is eligible for assessment based on current use [Arkansas Statutes Annotated, § 84-483]. The farmer, however, must apply to the county assessor for the use assessment [§ 84-484 (A)]. Determination of the eligibility of the land is made by the county board of equalization [§ 84-484 (B)].

Once land is classified under this act, it will continue to be so assessed provided the owner certifies its continued use as farm, agricultural, or timber land anually, until the land is withdrawn from farm, agricultural, or timber use [§ 84-484 (D)].

VALUATION

All lands which are actively devoted to farm, agricultural, or timber use will be assessed for ad valorem tax purposes on the basis of such current use, and not as if subdivided or on any other basis [§ 84-483].

CHANGE OF LAND USE

If the owner of such land should change its use from farm, agricultural, or timber use, he must notify the county assessor within 60 days [§ 84-484 (E)].

CALIFORNIA

The California farmland assessment law is of the contract type. Eligible farmers may enter into contracts with their city or county governments to restrict, for a period of at least 10 years, the use of their land to eligible agricultural and compatible open space uses. California law also provides for open space easements and scenic restrictions. In return, land is assessed according to capitalized income from its permitted use. Counties, cities, and school districts are reimbursed by the State in varying degrees for the tax revenue they lose.

The law, under which almost all of the restrictions making land eligible for use assessment are created, is known as the Williamson Act or the California Land Conservation Act of 1965. It has been amended frequently since its enactment. The most important amendments were made in 1969.

Farmland

DEFINITIONS

Agricultural commodity includes any plant and animal products produced for commercial purposes [Government Code, § 51201 (a)].

Agricultural use means using the land to produce an agricultural commodity for commercial purposes [§ 51201 (b)].

Prime agricultural land means any of the following: (1) land which is rated as class I or class II by the Soil Conservation Service; (2) land which is rated 80–100 on the Storie Index Rating; (3) land which supports livestock used for production of food and fiber if it has a minimum capacity of one animal unit per acre; (4) land planted with fruit or nut-bearing trees, vines, bushes, or crops which have a nonbearing period of less than 5 years and will normally return at least $200 per acre each year; (5) land which has produced unprocessed agricultural plants with an annual gross value of not less than $200 per acre for 3 of the 5 previous years [§ 51201 (c)].

An agricultural preserve may be an area devoted to agricultural use, recreational use, open space use, compatible uses, or any combination of these [§ 51201 (d)].

Compatible use is any use determined by the city or county governing body to be compatible with agricultural, recreational, or open space use of land [§ 51201 (e)].

Recreational use is the use of land by the public with or without charge for camping, picnicking, hiking, boating, hunting, swimming, or other outdoor sports. Any fee charged must be reasonable and may not unduly limit use of the land [§ 51201 (i)].

Open space use includes land maintained so as to preserve its natural characteristics, beauty, or openness for the enjoyment of the public, protection of wildlife, or production of salt as long as the land is in any of the following uses for which definitions are also provided in this section: scenic highway corridor, wildlife habitat area, saltpond, managed wetland area, and submerged area [§ 51201 (o)].

ESTABLISHMENT OF AGRICULTURAL PRESERVES

Agricultural preserves may be established by any city or county which has a general plan. The purpose of agricultural preserves is to designate the areas within which the city or county will be willing to enter into contracts, as defined in the next section. If land not under contract is included within the preserve, it must be restricted to compatible uses by zoning laws or other suitable means within 2 years [Government Code, Art. 2.5, § 51230-51233]. A proposal to establish an agricultural preserve must be submitted to the city or county planning commission for approval [§ 51234]. The city or county may later remove land from an agricultural preserve [§ 51236]. The annexation or incorporation of land in an agricultural preserve by a city does not affect the existence of the preserve except that the city then takes over the county's rights and responsibilities [§ 51235].

CONTRACTS

Any city or county may enter into contracts with respect to eligible land in agricultural preserves. The purpose of such a contract is to limit the use of the land for at least 10 years to preserve its agricultural or other open space use. A contract may provide for restrictions, terms, conditions, payments, and fees more restrictive than or in addition to those required by the State enabling legislation [§ 51240]. It will prohibit uses of the land for purposes other than agriculture and uses compatible with agriculture [§ 51243]. When the contract lasts for at least 10 years but less than 20 years, it is automatically extended for another year at each anniversary date unless notice of nonrenewal is given by either party shortly before the anniversary date [§ 51244]. Contracts for 20 years or more, however, may contain provisions for automatic extension only after expiration of up to 11 years of the contract term [§ 51244.5]. The contract will be binding on all successors in interest of the owner [§ 51243]. Once notice of nonrenewal has been given, then the existing contract will be in effect for the balance of the contract period [§ 51246].

CANCELLATION OF CONTRACT

The landowner may cancel a contract (as opposed to not renewing it) only if he can show the county board or city council that the cancellation is not inconsistent with the purpose of the act and that the cancellation is in the public interest. Existence of an opportunity for another use of the land or the uneconomic character of the existing agricultural use is not grounds for cancellation except under closely defined circumstances [§ 51282]. When cancellation is accomplished, the landowner will have to pay a can-

cellation fee equal to 12½ percent of the full cash value of the land after it
is free of the contractual restriction unless the fee is waived by the governing body with the approval of the secretary of the State resources agency
[§ 51283]. In case the contract was entered into prior to March 1, 1971, and
the county assessor subsequently changed the ratio of assessed to full cash
value, the cancellation fee is one-half the previously announced assessment ratio times the full cash value [§ 51283 (b)]. Cancellation will not
take place without a hearing [§ 51284].

Open Space Easements

Open space easements are created under a separate law [Government
Code, Chap. 6.5, § 51051-51052]. In granting such an easement, the owner
relinquishes to the public the right to construct improvements on the land
except as limited by the grant. These grants may be accepted by a city or a
county which has adopted a general plan. The easement and covenant
may not run for a period of less than 20 years [§ 51053].

ELIGIBILITY OF LAND FOR OPEN SPACE EASEMENTS

No grant of an open space easement may be accepted by a city or county
unless the appropriate governing body finds that: (a) the preservation of
this open space is consistent with the general plan of the city or county,
and is (b) for the enjoyment of scenic beauty, for use of natural resources,
for recreation, or for production of food and fiber [§ 51056]. In order for the
grant to be accepted, the city or county planning department must have
reported that it is consistent with the general plan [§ 51057].

IMPACT OF EASEMENT

Once the open space easement has been granted, no building permit may
be issued to allow the construction of a building which would violate the
easement [§ 51058].

ABANDONMENT OF EASEMENT

The government of a city or county may abandon an open space easement
if it and the planning commission determine that maintenance of the easement is no longer in the public interest. Accordingly, just prior to approval
of the abandonment resolution, the county assessor is to assess the open
space land at 25 percent of the fair market value it would have if it were
not covered by the easement, and the owner must pay 50 percent of the assessed value as a condition of abandoning the easement [§ 51061]. This
payment can be waived under certain circumstances.

Scenic Restrictions

A third law under which land can be restricted in ways that entitle it to use assessment authorizes counties and cities to acquire interests in real properties ". . . in order to preserve, through limitation of their future use, open spaces and areas for public use and enjoyment" [§ 6950]. Use assessment is available to such properties only when the restriction has an initial term of at least 10 years [Revenue and Taxation Code § 421].

Taxation

The constitution authorizes the legislature to define open space lands and to provide for their assessment on a basis that it determines to be consistent with their restriction and use when they are enforceably restricted to use for recreation, enjoyment of scenic beauty, natural resources, or production of food and fiber [Constitution, Art. XXVIII]. The enforceable restrictions to which this article applies now include: a Land Conservation Act contract, a Land Conservation Act agreement, a scenic restriction or an open space easement. No other types of restrictions on the use of land qualify the land for assessment on a basis other than market value [Revenue and Taxation Code, § 422].

VALUATION OF LAND SUBJECT TO OPEN SPACE RESTRICTION

In valuing land subject to an enforceable open space restriction, the county assessor must use the capitalization of income method and may not use sales data [§ 423].

Where sufficient rental information is available, the income will be the fair rent imputed to the land. The rent may be actually received by the owner or may be a rent typical of the area [§ 423 (a) (1)].

Where sufficient rental information is not available, the income will be what the land can be expected to yield under prudent management and subject to the enforceable restrictions. Income will be the difference between revenue and expenditures. A detailed method for determining revenue and expenditure is provided in the law [§ 423 (a) (2)].

A detailed method for determining an appropriate capitalization rate is also provided [§ 423 (b)]. It is based on an interest component equal to the yield on long-term U.S. government bonds, a risk component, a property tax component, and a component for amortization of an investment in perennials.

NONRENEWAL OF CONTRACT

Where notice of nonrenewal of a Land Conservation Act contract has been given by the owner, or by the governing body without protest by the owner, or where the owner has failed to give notice of renewal when it was due for scenic restrictions and open space easements, the assessor will reassess the land, and will do so each year until the contract expires [§ 426 (a)]. He will determine the full cash value of the land as if it were not subject to enforceable restriction. He then will determine the restricted use value of the land by the capitalization of income method, subtract this capitalized value from the unrestricted full cash value, and discount the difference at the yield rate of long-term U.S. government bonds for the number of years remaining in the contract. This last value will be added to the value derived by capitalization of income, and the assessed value will be 25 percent of the total [§ 426 (b)]. The same procedure applies for the last 5 years of a contract which is expiring by reason of a notice of nonrenewal given by the owner or protested by him.

Open Space Payments to Cities, Counties, and School Districts

The State provides payments (called "subventions" in the statute) to cities, counties, and school districts to compensate them in varying degrees for revenues lost because of the reduced property taxes paid on open space lands assessed pursuant to Sections 423 and 423.5 of the Revenue and Taxation Code [Government Code, § 16140-16141].

School districts can receive their subventions directly from the State [§ 16148-16152] and indirectly (as can special districts) through their constituent cities and counties [§ 16145].

The amount of the subvention is limited in two ways. These will be discussed later.

CITIES AND COUNTIES

The governing body of each county and city reports to the secretary of the resources agency, itemizing the number of acres of land it believes eligible for subventions. The secretary reviews the report and certifies the amount of the subvention to the controller [§ 16144]. He uses the following rates: (a) $3 for each acre of prime agricultural land in a city or within specific distances from a city, (b) $1.50 for all other prime agricultural land, and (c) $0.50 for all other land which is devoted to open space uses of statewide significance [§ 16142]. "Open space uses of statewide significance" means that the open space land either could be developed as prime agricultural land or is of more than local importance for ecological, economic, educational, or other purposes [§ 16143].

SCHOOL DISTRICTS

The assessor determines the "open space adjustment" for each school district in the county. This is the difference between the "adjusted assessed value" of all land in the district in the base year and the actual assessed value of all land in the district in the current year, excluding from both figures the assessed value of petroleum mineral rights. "Adjusted assessed value" is the actual assessed value of the land in the base year, exclusive of developed petroleum mineral rights, multiplied by the percentage by which the gross assessed value of all locally assessed land in the State outside municipalities changed in value (ignoring exemptions and deductions but including petroleum mineral rights) between the base year and the current year. The base year is the last year before differential assessment was applied to any land in the district. The State controller determines the statewide factors. If the local assessor was using an assessment ratio of less than 25 percent in the base year, then he must adjust his base year values to the 25 percent assessment ratio for subvention purposes [§ 16149].

The "open space adjustment" described above is multiplied by the amount by which the school district's tax rate exceeds the following: (a) $2.23 (per $100 assessed valuation) for an elementary school district, (b) $1.64 for a high school district, (c) $3.87 for a unified school district of grades K–12, and (d) $0.25 for a community college district [§ 16148]. The product of the "open space adjustment" and the excess tax rate will be the amount of the State subvention to the district [§ 16151].

LIMITATIONS

There is a limitation on subvention payments to cities and counties. For each property currently assessed as open space land pursuant to Section 423 or 423.5 of the Revenue and Taxation Code, the last assessment before it acquired an open space restriction (exclusive of the value of developed petroleum mineral rights) is multiplied by the statewide factor determined by the controller for school district subventions. The resulting figures for all restricted parcels in the city or county are added, and the sum is compared with the parcels' total current assessed value (exclusive of the value of developed petroleum mineral rights). The subvention for the current year cannot exceed the product of the current city or county tax rate times the amount of the aggregate decrease in assessed value thus computed [§ 16152].

The limitation on subventions to school districts is based on assessed value per pupil. No school district may receive aid if its actual assessed value per pupil is greater than the product of the "base year assessed value" per pupil and a ratio of the statewide current education expense per pupil to the statewide base year education expense per pupil. Nor may any school district receive more than specified amounts per acre of open space land (e.g., $1 per acre for a community college district receiving no State equalization aid [§ 16150].

Moreover, the total amount of subventions which the State controller may disburse cannot exceed an appropriate amount (e.g., $22 million in 1973–74). If claims by local governments exceed this limit, then subventions will be reduced on a pro-rata per acre basis, beginning with non-prime lands, then prime lands, and finally school districts [§ 16153].

REVENUE FACTOR ADJUSTMENT TAX

School districts with lands assessed under Section 423 or 423.5 of the Revenue and Taxation Code are authorized to levy a "revenue factor adjustment tax" which will produce an amount equal to (1) the tax rate for the district referred to in Section 16148 of the Government Code (see above) times the "open space adjustment" defined in Section 16149, minus (2) the difference between actual State aid (other than open space subventions) and the amount of such State aid the district would have received had its assessed value been equal to the adjusted assessed valuation described above. The revenue factor adjustment tax, however, may not exceed $.03 per $100 of assessed valuation [Education Code, § 20814.5].

COLORADO

Colorado enacted a preferential assessment law in 1967 and amended it in 1971 and 1973.

To be assessed as agricultural land, a parcel of land must be used presently and primarily to obtain profit by raising, harvesting, and selling crops or by the feeding, breeding, management, and sale of livestock, poultry, fur-bearing animals, honey bees, dairy stock, or their products, or for any other agricultural or horticultural use. The land must have been so used the preceding 2 years, and must also have been classified agricultural for the preceding 10 years [Colorado Revised Statutes, § 137-1-3 (6)].

The value of such agricultural land will be based on its earning or productive capacity during a reasonable period of time, capitalized at a rate of 11½ percent [§ 137-1-3 (5)].

CONNECTICUT

Connecticut enacted a differential assessment law in 1963. In 1972, the law was substantially amended to authorize a conveyance tax. Such a tax is collected in most cases when land which has been differentially assessed is sold or is changed to a higher use. The conveyance tax is not a true deferred tax but a new tax. Nevertheless, the Connecticut law more closely resembles a deferred tax than preferential assessment or a contract or agreement, so we have classified it as a deferred tax law.

DEFINITIONS

Farmland means any tract or tracts of land, including woodland and wasteland, constituting a farm unit [General Statutes of Connecticut, § 12-107b].

Forest land means any tract of land of 25 acres or more having tree growth in such quantity and so spaced and maintained as to constitute a forest in the opinion of the State forester [§ 12-107b].

Open space land means land whose preservation would enhance the conservation of natural, historic, and scenic resources; protect natural streams, water supply, wetlands, beaches, and soils; enhance the value of parks, forests, and wildlife preserves; create recreational opportunities; and promote orderly urban growth [§ 12-107b].

ELIGIBILITY

An owner of farmland may apply to the municipal assessor for its assessment as farmland. The assessor will determine if the land is farmland following such criteria as: acreage, portion of acreage in actual farm use, productivity, gross income, nature and value of equipment used on the land, and the extent to which the tracts comprising the unit are contiguous [§ 12-107c].

An owner of forest land must apply to the State forester for designation as forest land. If the State forester determines the land is indeed forest land, he will notify the owner and the appropriate assessor. The landowner then will apply to his local assessor for classification and taxation as forest land [§ 12-107d]. At a future date, the State forester may review the status of land designated forest land on his own initiative or at the assessor's request.

Open space land must be recommended for preservation and designated open space by a municipality's planning commission or similar agency in its plan of development. The owner of such land must apply for its classification as open space land in the assessment list. If the assessor determines that the land has retained its open space character, he will grant the open space classification [§ 12-107e].

VALUATION

The value of such agricultural, forest, or open space land will be based on its current use, without regard for neighborhood uses of a more intensive nature [§ 12-63].

CONVEYANCE TAX

Any land which has been classified as farm, forest, or open space will be subject to a conveyance tax if sold within 10 years from initial acquisition or classification. The tax is imposed in addition to the realty transfer tax. Its base is the total sale price of the land. The rates of the conveyance tax are as follows: 10 percent if sold within the first year of ownership or of classification, 9 percent if sold in the second year . . . and 1 percent if sold in the tenth year. No conveyance tax is due after the tenth year [Public Act 152, Laws of 1972, § 1, 5].

DELAWARE

Delaware enacted a preferential assessment law in 1968.

DEFINITIONS

Agricultural use means land devoted to the production for sale of plants and animals useful to man, such as: forage and sod crops, grains and feed crops, dairy animals and dairy products, poultry products, etc. [Delaware Code, § 8330 (c)].

Horticultural use means land devoted to the production for sale of fruits, vegetables, nursery, floral, and greenhouse products [§ 8330 (d)].

Forest use means land devoted to tree growth in such quantity and so spaced and maintained as to constitute in the opinion of the State forester a forest area [§ 8330 (e)].

ELIGIBILITY

Land must be at least 5 acres in area and have been actively devoted to agriculture, horticultural, or forest use for at least the 2 immediately preceding years; that is, gross sales must have averaged $500 per year for the 2 preceding years [§8330 (f)]. The landowner must apply [§ 8330 (g)].

VALUATION

Once the application is approved, then the value of the land for tax purposes will be based on its use in agricultural, horticultural, or forest use [§ 8330 (h)]. This will be determined by evidence of land capability, the assessor's own knowledge, and the recommendations of the State farmland advisory committee. This committee will annually determine a range of values for each of the several classifications of land in agricultural, horti-cultural, and forest use in various regions of the State. The committee will use the soil survey data and other evidences of land value [§ 8330 (m)].

FLORIDA

Florida's constitution was amended in 1968 to provide that agricultural land may be classified by general law and assessed only on the basis of its character or use. The history of differential assessment in that State goes back much earlier. The first differential assessment law was enacted in 1959. It was most recently revised in 1972. The law now provides for preferential assessment of farmland and restrictive covenants for taxation of outdoor recreational and park lands.

Farmland

DEFINITIONS

Bona fide agricultural purposes means good faith agricultural use of the land [Florida Statutes Annotated, § 193.461 (3) (b)].
Agricultural purposes include horticulture, floriculture, viticulture, pisci-culture, and other specified uses [§ 193.461 (5)].

ELIGIBILITY

The landowner must apply to the county assessor yearly. The assessor can classify the land as agricultural, using the following factors: (1) the length of time the land has been so utilized; (2) whether the land use has been continuous; (3) the purchase price paid; (4) size, as it relates to specific agricultural use; (5) whether an indicated effort has been made to care suf-ficiently and adequately for the land in accordance with accepted com-mercial agricultural practices, including fertilizing, liming, tilling, mowing, reforesting, and other accepted agricultural practices; and (6) whether the land is under lease and the effective length, terms, and condi-tions of the lease [§ 193.461 (3) (b)]. The assessor will reclassify the follow-ing lands as nonagricultural if: (1) the land has been diverted from agricultural to a nonagricultural use; (2) the land is no longer utilized for agricultural purposes; (3) the land has been zoned to a nonagricultural use at the request of the owner subsequent to the enactment of this law; or (4) the owner has recorded a subdivision plat for the land subsequent to the enactment of this law [§ 193.461 (4) (a)]. Land may also be reclassified non-agricultural if there is contiguous urban development and the agricultural land interferes with orderly expansion of the community [§ 193.461 (4) (b)]. Moreover, if the sale price of a piece of agricultural land is three or more times the agricultural assessment, tax authorities are instructed to presume that the land is not in bona fide agricultural use, unless the owner provides evidence to the contrary.

ASSESSMENT

Once proper application has been made and granted, the assessor will assess the land considering the following factors: (1) size and quantity of the property; (2) the condition of the property; (3) the present market value of the land in agriculture; (4) the income produced from the land; (5) the present productivity of the land; and (6) the economic merchantability of the agricultural product [§ 193.461 (6) (a)].

If the proper application has not been made or the approval not been granted, then the land shall be assessed as all other land [§ 193.461 (6) (b)].

Outdoor Recreational and Park Lands

DEFINITIONS AND ELIGIBILITY

Some outdoor recreational purposes are boating, golfing, camping, swimming, and horseback riding, and historical, archaeological, scenic, or scientific sites. A development right is the right of any owner to change the use of the land to anything but outdoor recreational or park purposes [§ 193.501 (6) (a), (b)].

DEVELOPMENT RIGHTS AND COVENANTS

The owner in fee of any land which is used for outdoor recreational or park purposes may convey the development right of that land to the governing board of a county or he may covenant with the governing board of the county for a period of at least 10 years to keep that land for outdoor recreational or park purposes [§ 193.501 (1) (a), (b)]. Likewise, the county board is authorized to accept the development rights or establish such a covenant [§ 193.501 (2) (a), (b)].

ASSESSMENT

When the development rights have been conveyed or the land has been put under covenant, the land will be eligible for assessment according to its value in its present use. If a covenant extends for less then 10 years, the land will be assessed according to its market value [§ 193.011] as restricted by the covenant [§ 193.501 (3)]. During the life of the covenant, the landowner may not change the use of the land without the consent of the county governing board, who must first reconvey the development right of the owner or release the owner from the terms of the covenant. The reconveyance or release will be contingent upon the owner's payment of any deferred taxes. The amount of deferred tax will be equal to the difference between taxes which would have been paid had the land been assessed at its market value, and the taxes actually paid, plus 6 percent interest. The period of the deferred tax is the length of time the conveyance or the convent was in effect [§ 193.501 (4)].

HAWAII

In 1961, Hawaii enacted a law concerning the tax assessment of agricultural land and revised it in 1967, 1969, and 1973. In 1969, similar laws were enacted for golf courses and for residences of taxpayers 60 years old or older. The differential assessment of farmland, golf courses, and some residences is only one of the provisions of Hawaii law which deals with land use, planning, zoning, and economic growth. This law is based on the dedication of land to these select uses and is classified in this report in the restrictive agreements category. The 1973 amendments extended differential assessment to agricultural lands which are not dedicated lands. In this case, deferred taxation is used.

Hawaii law provides for the establishment of a land use commission [Hawaii Revised Statutes, § 205-1], which is charged with classifying and setting boundaries for all lands in the State according to the following categories: (1) urban districts, (2) rural districts, (3) agricultural districts, and (4) conservation districts [§ 205-2]. Zoning ordinances will be based on these land classifications [§ 205-5]. In establishing the boundaries of agricultural districts, the greatest possible protection shall be given to those lands with a high capacity for intensive cultivation.

Agricultural districts include uses such as the cultivation of crops, orchards, forage and forestry; farming activities or uses related to animal husbandry, game, and fish propagation; services and uses accessory to the above activities including, but not limited to, living quarters or dwellings, mills, storage facilities, processing facilities, and roadside stands for the sale of products grown on the premises, and open area recreational facilities [§ 205-2]. Certain other compatible uses may be permitted by zoning ordinances [§ 205-5].

Rural districts include activities or uses as characterized by low density residential lots mixed with small farms [§ 205-2].

In determining the value of land other than land classified and used for agriculture, consideration is to be given to: selling prices and income (including such data on comparable property), productivity, nature of use (actual and potential), location, accessibility, etc. [§ 246-10 (f)]. Records are to be kept in each district to show the methods established to determine value [§ 246-10 (c)].

Dedicated Lands

The sections of the law applying to dedicated lands provide for differential assessment of farmland, livestock use land, golf courses, and residential land. An owner of an eligible parcel of land may dedicate his land to ranching, livestock use, agricultural use, golf course use, or residential use. The method for reducing taxes will depend on the number of years the dedication will be in effect.

ELIGIBILITY OF AGRICULTURAL LAND

Dedicated lands may be located in any of the four districts. If the agricultural land is in an urban district, it must currently be and substantially and continuously have been used for the cultivation of crops such as sugar cane, pineapple, truck crops, orchard crops, ornamental crops, or the like for the 5-year period preceding the dedication request [§ 246-12 (a)]. If the land is in an agricultural district, it may be dedicated for a 20-year period [§ 246-12 (a)].

The owner of land in agricultural or ranching use must petition the director of taxation, who will then have the State department of agriculture determine whether the land is reasonably well suited for its intended use, using such criteria as productivity ratings, ownership, size of operating unit, and present use of surrounding similar lands. The director of planning and economic development will at the same time determine whether the intended use is in conflict with the overall development plan of the State. If the land is in an urban district, the director will further determine the economic feasibility of the intended use of the land. If the petition is approved, then the landowner forfeits the right to change the use of the land for the next 10 or 20 years. Should the land use district be changed to urban, then the agreement may be cancelled. Otherwise, notice of nonrenewal may be given after the ninth year for a 10-year dedication or the nineteenth year for a 20-year dedication with expiration to come 1 year after [§ 246-12].

VALUATION OF AGRICULTURAL LAND

If the petition is accepted, and the land is located in an agricultural district and it is dedicated for 20 years, then the land will be taxed at 50 percent of its assessed value in such use [§ 246-12 (a)]. If, however, the land is dedicated for 10 years, then it will be taxed on its full assessed value in agricultural or ranching use [§ 246-12 (b)].

FAILURE TO OBSERVE AGREEMENT

Should the owner fail to restrict use of the land in accordance with the agreement, then the special tax assessment will be cancelled retroactive to the date of the dedication. Deferred taxes equal to the difference between taxes actually paid and taxes which would have been paid had the land not been dedicated, plus a 10 percent per year penalty calculated from each year that taxes were deferred, will be collected. The State may use other remedies to enforce the agreement [§ 246-12 (d)].

ELIGIBILITY OF LIVESTOCK USE LAND

An owner of land within an urban district may dedicate his land for a specific livestock use such as feedlots, calf raising, and like operations in dairy, beef, swine, poultry, and aquaculture, but excluding grazing or pasturing, and have his land assessed in such use. The land must have been substantially and continuously in such use. It must also be compatible with surrounding uses [Act 175, Laws 1973, Section 3].

ELIGIBILITY OF GOLF COURSE LAND

The owner of a golf course must petition the director of taxation to have his land dedicated to golf course use. As a precondition to his petition being granted, he must agree not to discriminate against an individual using the golf course because of the individual's race, sex, religion, color, or ancestry [§ 246-12.2 (2)]. Approval of the petition to dedicate the land will mean the owner will forfeit any right to change the use of the land for at least 10 years, automatically renewable indefinitely. The dedication petition may be cancelled by either party once 5 years' notice is given.

VALUATION OF GOLF COURSE LAND

If the petition is approved, then the golf course land will be assessed on the basis of its value as a golf course. Some factors to be considered are rental income, cost of development, sales price, and the effect of the value of the golf course on the value of surrounding land.

If the landowner changes the golf course use to another use, in violation of the restrictions, then the special tax assessment will be cancelled retroactive to the date of the petition up to a maximum of 10 years. The difference in the taxes actually paid and the taxes which would have paid had the land been in the higher use plus 6 percent penalty will be due for each year up to the time limitation. The State may use other means to enforce the covenant [§ 246-12.2 (1) (A), (B), (C)].

ELIGIBILITY OF RESIDENTIAL LAND

An owner or lessor with a 10-year lease, who is 60 years of age or older, is eligible to dedicate his real property to residential use. The land must be 10,000 square feet, be in an urban district, be used for single-family residential use, and be used by the owner or lessor as his home. Only one parcel of land may be dedicated for residential use by any owner. The owner or lessor must apply to the director of taxation. If the petition is accepted, then the land use is limited to its current restricted use. The period of the restriction is for 10 years into the future. Either party may cancel after 5 years.

VALUATION OF RESIDENTIAL LAND

If the petition is approved, then the land will be valued only according to its value as a residence.

Failure to restrict the land to its dedicated use will subject the owner to roll-back taxes plus an 8 percent penalty. The roll-back will be due from the date of the original petition. There is no maximum for the period of the roll-back [§ 246-12.3].

Deferred Taxes

CLASSIFICATION OF LAND

Land in each county will be classified according to its highest and best use as follows [§ 246-10 (d) (1)]:

Category I
  (A) improved residential
  (B) agricultural
  (C) conservation

Category II
  (D) unimproved residential
  (E) hotel and apartment

Category III
  (F) commercial

Category IV
  (G) industrial

In assigning land to one of these categories, the director of taxation will give major consideration to the land use commission's districting system (described above), the county planning and zoning ordinance, and use classifications in the State general plan [§ 246-10 (d) (2)].

VALUATION

In determining the value of lands classified and used for agriculture, whether dedicated or not, the assessor will consider rent, productivity, nature or actual agricultural use, advantages or disadvantages of factors such as location, accessibility, transportation facilities, size, shape, topography, quality of soil, water privileges, availability of water and its cost, easements and appurtenances, and the opinions of persons who have special knowledge of land values [§ 246-10 (2) (f) (2)].

DEFERRED TAXES

When land has been assessed according to its agricultural use as provided immediately above, and the classification of the land is changed to urban or rural district, or the land is subdivided into parcels of 5 acres or less, then deferred taxes will be due. The time span of the deferred taxes will be from the year agricultural use assessment was first applied but will be no longer than 10 years. The amount of deferred taxes will be based on the difference between the assessed value at its highest and best use and its assessed value in agricultural use, at the tax rate applicable for the appropriate years. Deferred taxes will not be collected if the landowner dedicates his land within 1 year of a change in land use classification [§ 246-10 (2) (f) (3)].

IDAHO

In 1971, Idaho enacted a law which has a bearing on use assessment of farmland. It provides that actual and functional use will be a major consideration when determining the market value of commerical and agricultural land [Idaho Code, § 63-202].

ILLINOIS

Illinois amended its constitution in 1970 to allow the legislature to provide for deferred taxation. Interest, at 5 percent, is charged on the deferred tax.

ELIGIBILITY

Real property is considered used for farming or agricultural purposes if ". . . it is more than 10 acres in area and devoted primarily to the raising and harvesting of crops; to the feeding, breeding, and management of livestock . . . with the intention of securing substantial income from these activities." Land in Federal programs will count toward achieving eligibility. The land must have been in farm use for 3 years prior to the filing of application for farm use assessment [Illinois Annotated Statutes, § 501a-1]. The person liable for taxes will file a verified application with the county assessor who will then determine if the application meets the requirements [§ 502a-2].

When the land assessed under this law is no longer used for farming, the person liable for taxes must so notify the assessor [§ 502a-2].

METHOD OF ASSESSMENT

Assessment will be made on the basis of the price the land would bring at a fair voluntary sale for farm use [§ 501a-1]. The valuation so determined will be repeated every year that the owner applies and meets the eligibility criteria [§ 501a-3].

DEFERRED TAXES

When land is no longer used for farming purposes, the person liable for taxes will pay, for the preceding 3 years, the difference between taxes actually paid and taxes which would otherwise have been paid plus 5 percent interest [§ 501a-3].

INDIANA

Indiana enacted a preferential assessment law in 1961. The statute provides that land devoted to agricultural use will be assessed as agricultural land as long as it is in agricultural use. Agricultural use assessment does not apply to land purchased for industrial, commercial, or residential uses [Indiana Statutes Annotated, § 64-711b]. In valuing land used for agriculture, the county assessor will appoint a committee of five persons, at least two of whom are agricultural landowners in the county, to help determine land values. This will be known as the county land advisory committee. The indicators of value determined by this committee will be used as guides in determining value of agricultural land [§ 64-712].

IOWA

Iowa has a preferential assessment law, enacted in 1967 and amended in 1968 and 1969. It has an unusual limit on the rate of taxation of farmland within municipal boundaries.

AGRICULTURAL LAND WITHIN CORPORATE LIMITS

To be eligible under this provision, land must be within the limits of a municipal corporation, must be larger than 10 acres, and must be used in good faith for agricultural or horticultural purposes. It may not be taxed at a rate greater than one and one-fourth mills and then only for municipal street purposes [Iowa Code Annotated, § 404.15].

ASSESSMENT OF AGRICULTURAL LAND

In determining the actual value of agricultural property, the assessor will consider equally (1) the productivity and net earning capacity determined on the basis of agricultural use, capitalized at a rate considered by the State board of tax review to be a fair return on the investment, and (2) the fair and reasonable market value of such property based ". . . only on its current use and not on its potential value for other uses" [§ 441.21].

KENTUCKY

Kentucky has a deferred tax law for agricultural and horticultural land. The constitutional amendment authorizing the deferred taxation of land in agricultural or horticultural use was approved in 1969. In 1970, the general assembly enacted implementing legislation effective January 1, 1971.

DEFINITIONS

Agricultural land means a tract of land of at least 10 contiguous acres used to produce livestock, poultry, tobacco, timber, and other crops. The average gross income from the land must have been at least $1,000 per year for the 2 preceding years, or there must be evidence that it will average this amount. Payments for land which meets the requirements for State and Federal agricultural programs may be counted in the average gross income. Land devoted to growing timber for market is excluded from the gross income provision [Kentucky Revised Statutes, § 132.010 (7)].

   Horticultural land means a tract of land of at least 5 contiguous acres commerically used for the cultivation of a garden or orchard or to raise fruits, vegetables, flowers, or ornamentals. The average gross income from these activities must have averaged $1,000 per year for the past 2 years, or there must be evidence that it will average this amount [§ 132.010 (8)].

Agricultural or horticultural value is determined by ". . . representative sale prices of comparable land purchased for agricultural or horticultural use with consideration being given to the purpose of purchase, such as farm expansion, improved accessibility and other like factors unduly influencing the sale price" [§ 132.010 (9)].

ELIGIBILITY

Land must have been in these uses for at least 5 successive years, and the property valuation administrator must have placed a value on the land greater than its agricultural or horticultural value [§ 132.450 (2) (a)]. Specifically excluded is land zoned for other than agricultural or horticultural use and land owned by a corporation organized for other than strictly agricultural or horticultural purposes [§ 132.450 (2) (b), (c)]. The landowner must apply [§ 132.450 (2) (a)].

DEFERRED TAX

When a change in land use occurs, the landowner must pay the amount of the deferred tax for the 2-year period preceding the change [§ 132.450 (f)]. The amount of a deferred tax is the difference between a tax based on agricultural or horticultural value and a tax based on fair cash value [§ 132.010 (9), (10)].

MAINE

Maine amended its constitution in 1970 enabling the legislature to enact laws pertaining to the current use assessment of farmland, timberland, open space land used for recreation or scenic beauty, and lands used for game and wildlife sanctuaries. A deferred tax law was enacted in 1971 to carry out the farmland and open space objectives of the amendment. The "Tree Growth Tax Law" was enacted in 1972 and amended in 1973 to do the same for forest land.

Farm and Open Space Land

DEFINITIONS

Farmland means any tract or tracts of land including woodland and wasteland making up a farm unit of at least 10 contiguous acres producing a gross income of at least $1,000 per year for 3 of the preceding 5 years [1971 Regular Session Laws, Chap. 548, Subchapter 11-B, § 586].

Open space lands include land in wildlife management areas and preserves and farmland, the preservation of which would preserve scenic resources, enhance public recreational opportunities, promote game management, or preserve wildlife.

ELIGIBILITY OF FARMLAND

An owner of land may file an application with the municipal tax assessor or State tax assessor, as appropriate, who will determine whether such land is to be identified as farmland on the assessment list. The factors to be considered are: acreage, portion in actual farm use, productivity, gross income derived from the land, nature and value of equipment employed on the land, and extent to which the tracts of land are contiguous.

ELIGIBILITY OF OPEN SPACE LAND

The planning board of a municipality may prepare a comprehensive plan and designate land for preservation as open space land. An owner of land in an area so designated may then apply for this classification [§ 588].

SCENIC EASEMENTS

A municipality may acquire scenic easements or development rights to preserve property in farm or open space use. The minimum term will be for 10 years [§ 589].

VALUATION

The valuation of any land classified as farm or open space land will be based on its current use as determined by the State tax assessor. Municipal tax assessors may or may not use these values. If they do not, they must be prepared to explain their valuation system [§ 590].

RECAPTURE PENALTY

Any change in land use which disqualifies land for the above classifications shall cause a penalty to be assessed against the land. This penalty will be equal to the total amount of taxes which would have been paid had land been valued at its highest and best use, in each of the years it had the special classification, less all taxes which were paid, plus 8 percent annual interest.

The maximum time span of the recapture penalty for open space lands is 15 years; for farmland, 10 years [§ 591].

LIMIT ON ACREAGE

A person may not apply for classification for more than 15,000 acres [§ 593].

Tree Growth Tax Law

DEFINITION

Forest land means land used primarily for the growth of trees and forest products but does not mean the ledges, marshes, open swamps, bogs, water, and similar areas which may be found within forest lands [Maine Revised Statutes Annotated, § 573, sub-§ 3].

ELIGIBILITY

The provisions of this law have mandatory application to forest land of more than 500 acres. The owner or owners of forest land between 10 and 500 acres may apply [§ 574].

VALUATION

The State tax assessor will determine the proportions of various tree species and various forest products for each forest type. He will need this figure to determine the "average annual net wood production rates" and "average stumpage values" for each forest type in each county [§ 576]. From the results of growth rate surveys are calculated the "average annual net wood production rates," which are reduced by 30 percent, the rate which supports sustained logging [§ 576]. The value of the "annual net wood production" for a forest type in a county is equal to the "average annual net wood production rate" per acre for a forest type, multiplied by the weighted average of the stumpage values of all species in the type [§ 573, sub-§ 9]. This value of "annual net wood production" for each forest type in each county is capitalized at a 10 percent rate, to produce the 100 percent valuation figure used by assessors to value forest land [§ 576]. The assessor who is responsible for any eligible forest land will adjust the 100 percent valuation by the local assessment ratio to obtain the assessed value of the forest land.

ELIGIBILITY FOR STATE AID

Following the first year the law is in effect, if the forest valuation scheme reduces the total assessed valuation of all land in a municipality by more than 10 percent, then the municipality will have a valid claim against the

State to recover the lost taxes. Such claims will be presented to the State legislature next convening [§ 578, sub-§ 1]. However, for the first year of valuation under this act, in organized and unorganized areas, if the total assessed valuation has been reduced by more than 10 percent from the year before, then the forest valuation will be adjusted back so that the reduction is not more than 10 percent [§ 578, sub-§ 1-2].

CHANGE IN LAND USE

The landowners must report any change in land use. If they fail to do so, the assessor will collect taxes which should have been paid, deferred taxes for up to the previous 5 years, plus 25 percent penalty on the deferred taxes.

If land is reclassified, at the owner's or assessor's initiative, then the owner has two alternative ways of paying taxes. In the first case, deferred taxes for up to 5 years will be due plus interest charged from the year the taxes were deferred. In the second case, the amount of tax due will be equal to the amount by which the fair market valuation exceeds the 100 percent forest use valuation, multiplied by 10 percent up to the year 1978, 20 percent up to the year 1983, and 30 percent thereafter [§ 581, 581-A, 581-B].

FOREST LAND VALUATION ADVISORY COUNCIL

This council will be made up of the State forest commissioner, and a municipal officer, a forest landowner, and a citizen with a background in economics. It will advise the State tax assessor about administering this law.

MARYLAND

Maryland first enacted a preferential assessment law in 1956. A constitutional amendment was approved in 1960 after the courts had declared sections of the law unconstitutional.

The current law provides for a combination of preferential assessment, deferred taxation, and tax agreements for agricultural lands, woodlands, country club land, and land planned and zoned for satellite cities.

Agricultural Land

DEFINITION AND ELIGIBILITY

Definition and eligibility are to be determined by the State department of assessments and taxation. In determining whether lands which appear to be in farm use are in fact bona fide farms, it may use these criteria: (1) zoning applicable to the land, (2) present and past use of the land, and (3) productivity of the land [Annotated Code of Maryland, Art, 81, § 19 (b) (1)].

VALUATION

Agricultural lands which meet the eligibility requirements will be assessed on the basis of their farm use and not as if subdivided [§ 19 (b) (1)].

DEFERRED TAXES

No land which has been assessed on the basis of agricultural use may be developed for nonagricultural use for a 3-year period after the last year the land was thus taxed, unless the owner pays an amount equal to twice the difference between the taxes based of agricultural value and the taxes based on full value in the year development begins. Building permits will not be issued until the assessor certifies these conditions have been met [§ 19 (b) (2) (i), (ii)].

Woodland

DEFINITION AND ELIGIBILITY

Land eligible for this program must be a tract of at least 5 acres. The owner may enter into an agreement with the department of forests and parks to place his land in the program of forest conservation and management [Art. 66C, § 411-½ (c)]. The time period and conditions of the agreement will be determined by the department.

ASSESSMENT OF WOODLAND

As long as the land is under contract, its assessment for State, county, special tax district, and municipal taxes will not be increased [§ 411-½ (d)].

DEFERRED TAXES

When the contract time period lapses, or if all the timber is harvested, or if the tract is sold to a new owner, then the land will be reassessed. If the new valuation is greater than the old one, then the difference will be divided into a number of equal annual steps corresponding to the number of years the contract existed. Taxes will be due on the increases and will be calculated at the tax rates applicable to the particular years [§ 411-½ (f)].

TRANSFERABILITY OF CONTRACT

A buyer of land under contract may also acquire and assume the obligations of the contract. Under this condition, he will not have to pay deferred taxes at this time [§ 411-½ (h)].

Country Clubs

DEFINITION AND ELIGIBILITY

A country club is an area of land of at least 50 acres, ". . . on which is maintained a regular or championship golf course of nine holes or more and a clubhouse, and which has a dues paying membership . . ." of at least ". . . one hundred persons who pay dues averaging at least $50 annually per person. The use of the club will be restricted to members, their families and guests . . ." but the use of the club facilities by other than members and guests will not disqualify a club [Art. 81, § 19 (e) (4)].

AGREEMENT

Country clubs and the State department of assessments and taxation may enter into uniform agreements to assess and tax the eligible land only on the basis of its use as a country club and not as if it were subdivided or used for any other purpose [§ 19 (e) (1), (2)]. The time period of the agreement will be for a minimum of 10 years and may be extended in increments of 5 years [§ 19 (e) (5), (7), (14)]. When the full cash valuation of the land is greater than the country club use valuation, then the assessor will record both valuations. If the property under agreement subsequently is sold or no longer meets the definition of country club before the expiration date of the agreement, then back taxes will be collected. The amount of taxes will be determined for each appropriate year by applying the tax rate against the difference between the two assessments and summing the taxes for each year. The time limit for deferred taxation is 10 years [§ 19 (e) (7)].

Planned Development Lands

DEFINITION AND ELIGIBILITY

Land to be assessed and taxed as planned development land must be in an area covered by a current master plan or otherwise designated as a satellite city or town. Such plans must be approved by the government planning or zoning agency having jurisdiction. It must also be zoned for the development approved in the master plan. The zoning classification must have a comprehensive site development plan considering land use, utility requirements, highway needs, water and sewers, industrial use, job opportunities, recreation, and civic life. The owners of the land so zoned must pay for streets, open spaces, parks, school sites, and other property needed for public use. The tract of land must be contiguous and be at least 500 acres in size. At the time of zoning, the land must be primarily undeveloped. The owner must apply [Art. 81, § 19 (f) (1), (2), (3)].

ASSESSMENT

If the assessor approves the application, then the land will be assessed at a rate equal to the rate applied to lands in agricultural use, regardless of whether it meets the criteria for agricultural use assessment [§ 19 (f) (3)]. If the full cash value assessment is greater than the special assessment, then the assessor will record both valuations.

CHANGE IN LAND USE

When a portion of land under this special assessment is subdivided by the recording of a subdivision plat or permanent buildings are constructed on it, then that portion of the land will subsequently be taxed according to its full cash value. The rest of the undeveloped land will continue to receive the special assessment, even if it is less than 500 acres [§ 19 (f) (5)]. However, if the owner should initiate a rezoning classification that is not approved in the master plan, then the special assessment will terminate and back taxes will be collected. The amount of back taxes will be equal to the difference between the taxes which would have been paid based on full cash value assessment and the taxes actually paid based on the special assessment for each year the special assessment existed. The limit on the amount of the deferred tax is 10 percent of the full cash value assessment [§ 19 (f) (6)].

MASSACHUSETTS

In 1972, Massachusetts voters approved an amendment to the State constitution permitting the general court to enact laws on the assessment of agricultural or horticultural land at its value in those uses. At the time this bulletin was written, the legislature had not passed implementing legislation [Annotated Laws of Massachusetts, Constitution].

MICHIGAN

In 1973, a bill which applied the circuit breaker principle to the taxation of farmland was introduced in the Michigan legislature. A circuit breaker typically provides for a tax rebate or credit to eligible farmers for that portion of real property taxes which exceeds a given percentage of farm income. Even though the circuit breaker approach is not yet law, we think it is potentially important enough to merit description here. In addition, this bill has elements of a restrictive agreement.

ELIGIBILITY

Eligible owners of farmland must be either "natural persons" (i.e., not a corporation), a partnership, an agricultural corporation taxed under Subchapter S of the Internal Revenue Code of the United States, or joint tenants among family members [Senate Substitute for House Bill 4244, 1973 session, Michigan legislature, § 1 (b)].

A contract may be entered into by an eligible owner of agricultural land and the Michigan department of treasury to keep that land in agricultural use for 10 years [§ 1]. The land must meet one of the following requirements: (1) A farm of 40 or more acres must have been devoted primarily to agricultural or horticultural use during 3 of the 5 preceding years. The farm must continue in this use while in the contract program [§ 2 (a)]. (2) A farm of between 5 and 40 acres devoted primarily to agricultural or horticultural use must have produced a gross income of $100 or more per year per acre during 3 of the preceding 5 years. The farm must continue in this use while in the program [§ 2 (b)]. (3) A farm designated as a speciality farm by the State department of agriculture must have produced a gross income from agriculture or horticulture of $2,000 per year for 3 of the preceding 5 years. The farm must continue in this use while in the program [§ 2 (c)].

Other eligibility requirements are that any noncontiguous land must have been an integral part of farm operations for 3 of the 5 preceding years; no land in residential, commercial, or industrial use (except the farm homestead) may be included; and the land must have adequate drainage and soil depth for agricultural or horticultural operations [§ 2 (e)].

The State department of the treasury must accept an application for a contract unless (1) the land is wholly or partially unsuited for agricultural use as described above, or (2) the land is wholly or partially zoned for high density uses [§ 3].

CONTRACT PROVISIONS

A standard contract is prescribed which includes the following provisions: (1) Only reasonably needed farm structures may be built on the land. (2)

Only land improvements reasonably needed for farm operations may be made. (3) The only interests in the land that can be sold will be those which do not hinder farm operations, i.e., scenic, access, or utility easements. (4) For a farm of more than 40 acres, a drop in intensity of use below $10,000 per year gross receipts in 3 out of 5 years will constitute a violation of the contract unless it results from natural disaster; crop, structure, equipment, or livestock loss; a fall in market price; or compliance with Federal production restrictions. (5) If any of these provisions are violated or the ownership is transferred and the new owner fails to enter into the contract, then the applicant will pay a penalty of 100 percent of the current State equalized value of the land and structures in the year the change occurs. If the transfer is by sale, the penalty will be 100 percent of the equalized value or 50 percent of the sales price, whichever is greater [§ 5].

CIRCUIT BREAKER

The owner of land and buildings under contract will receive a credit against his State income tax liability equal to the amount by which his real property taxes exceeds 8 percent of household income. The limit on the credit is $3,000 per year [§ 7 (1)].

SPECIAL ASSESSMENTS

Special assessments for sewer, water, lights, or nonfarm drainage may only be imposed on a half acre lot surrounding a dwelling or other nonfarm structure if the land is under contract. Moreover, before the rest of the land under contract may use any improvements financed by special assessments, the owner must pay an amount equal to what would have been paid had the land not been exempted [§ 8 (3)].

MINNESOTA

Minnesota enacted its deferred tax law in 1967 and amended it in 1969 and 1973.

DEFINITIONS

Agricultural use land is defined as land from which the owner derives a third of the total family income or from which the total production income is $300 per year plus $10 per tillable acre. The land must be devoted to the production for sale of livestock, dairy products, horticultural and nursery stock, forage, grain, fur-bearing animals, bees, apiary products, etc. [Minnesota Statutes Annotated, § 273.111, Subd. 6].

Private outdoor recreational, open space, and park land for tax deferment purposes includes land devoted exclusively to golf or skiing and other related recreational uses. It must be at least 5 acres in size and either (1) be operated privately and open to the public, (2) be operated by firms for the benefit of their employees and guests, or (3) be operated by private clubs having a membership of at least 50 people [§ 273.112, Subd. 3].

ELIGIBILITY

Agricultural use land must be at least 10 acres in size. It must also be either the homestead of the owner or the owner's spouse, siblings, or children, or it must have been in the possession of the owner or his immediate family for at least 7 years prior to application. A family farm corporation, if it meets all other requirements, will be eligible if all stockholders are members of a family related to each other within the third degree of kindred [§ 273.111, Subd. 3].

The owner of the agricultural and private outdoor recreational, open space, and park land must apply to the assessor for the special valuation. Once application has been approved, it shall continue in effect until the property no longer qualifies [§ 273.111, Subd. 4, 8].

VALUATION

In determining agricultural use value, the assessor will not consider any added values resulting from nonagricultural factors [§ 273.111, Subd. 4]. Instead, he will consider its earning potential as measured by its free market rental rate [§273.12]. He will note the market value separately and will determine the mill rate applicable to such property.

The value of real estate in the eligible open space uses will be determined only with reference to its value in those uses. The assessor will not consider the value such real estate would have if it were converted to commercial, industrial, residential, or seasonal residential use [§ 273.112, Subd. 4]. The assessor will record the market value of the land separately.

DEFERRED TAXES

Once property has been valued and taxed as described above, and it is sold or its use changes and the land no longer qualifies, then deferred taxes will be due. The amount will be the difference between taxes paid and those that would have been paid had market value been the sole criterion for assessment. Such taxes will be collected only for the preceding 3 years for agricultural land [§ 273.111, Subd. 9] and 7 years for open space land [§ 273.112, Subd. 7].

MONTANA

In 1957, Montana enacted a law classifying all lands in the State. Agricultural land was graded and each grade was assessed using a rate determined by the State board of equalization. Montana enacted a deferred tax law in 1973.

ELIGIBILITY

Land will be eligible for valuation according to its productive capacity each year it meets the following qualifications: (1) it is actively devoted to agriculture, and (2) it is either at least 5 acres in size, and the gross value of its production is at least $1,000 per year, or it produces at least 15 percent of the owner's income. The owner must apply [Montana Session Laws, Chap. 512, § 4].

VALUATION

Land which the county assessor has determined to be in agricultural use will be valued according to its productive capacity [Revised Code of Montana, § 84-401] and not according to the best and highest use of neighboring lands [§ 84-429.12.1]. The State department of revenue will provide a general and uniform method of classifying lands. Each class of land will be graded according to its soil and productive capacity [§ 84-429.12].

DEFERRED TAX

Once land has been valued and taxed under this law, and its use is changed, then it will be liable for a roll-back tax for up to the preceding 4 years [MSL, Chap. 512, § 6]. The amount of the roll-back is determined by multiplying the full and fair value of the land, as reclassified according to its new use, by the number of years in the roll-back and applying the assessment ratio against that product. The resulting figure is multiplied by the average mill levy for the years included in the roll-back period, and the taxes actually paid are then subtracted from it [§ 6] to give the amount of the roll-back tax.

NEBRASKA

Nebraska amended its constitution in November 1972 to enable the legislature to enact laws providing that the value of land actively devoted to agriculture or horticulture would be its value in those uses, without regard to its potential value in other uses. To date, the legislature has not done so [Nebraska Constitution, Art. VIII, § 1].

NEVADA

Nevada presently does not have a differential assessment law on the books. One was enacted in 1961 and later declared unconstitutional by the courts.

The legislature, in its 56th session, passed a resolution to amend Section 1 of Article 10 of the State constitution. The resolution then also passed the 1973 legislature as required. It will now be submitted to the electorate to be voted upon in 1974.

The proposed amendment permits the legislature to classify open space and agricultural real property separately for tax purposes. The legislature will also provide for 7 years' retroactive assessment should land use be changed to a higher use.

NEW HAMPSHIRE

New Hampshire amended its constitution in 1968 to enable the legislature to provide for tax valuations based on use [New Hampshire Revised Statutes Annotated, Pt. 2, Art. 5-B]. Between 1968 and 1973, when new permanent legislation was enacted, New Hampshire had some temporary laws which provided for the taxation of farm and forest land.

The 1973 law, to be effective April 1974, has two parts—deferred taxes and restrictive agreements. The deferred tax is not a true deferred tax but a new tax imposed when land use changes. Nevertheless, it more closely resembles a deferred tax than preferential assessment or a contract or agreement. We have, therefore, classified it as a deferred tax law. The restrictive agreements are based on the acquisition of discretionary easements by local government.

Purpose of this law is to preserve open space in the State by providing a healthful and attractive outdoor environment for work and recreation by maintaining the character of the State's landscape and by conserving the land, water, forest, and wildlife resources. The means for preserving open space are current-use assessment and the acquisition of discretionary easements [§ 79-A:1].

Current Use Taxation

DEFINITIONS

Farmland means land devoted to agriculture or horticulture. The commissioner of agriculture will develop further criteria which the current use advisory board will adopt [§ 79-A:2 III].

Flood plain means undeveloped flood plains as determined by the flood plains commission and the current use advisory board [§ 79-A:2 IV].

Forest land means any land receiving silvicultural treatment. The State forester and current use advisory board will develop further criteria [§ 79-A:2 V].

Open space land means any farmland, forest land, wetland, recreational land, flood plain, or wild land and any undeveloped or unoccupied land that is so designated by action of a town or city for a period of at least 10 years. Recreational land means any undeveloped land open to public recreational use without entrance fee. Further criteria are determined by the State director of parks and the director of fish and game and adopted by the current use advisory board. Wetland means a marsh, swamp, or bog subject to flooding including the surrounding shore and including any soil designated as poorly drained by the national cooperative soil survey or as determined by criteria developed by the current use advisory board. Wild land means any unimproved land upon which there are no detrimental structures and on which the owner is not interfering with natural ecological processes as determined by the criteria of the current use advisory board [§ 79-A:2 VII, X, XI, XII].

ELIGIBILITY

The owner must apply for the special classification to the local tax officials. Each year the tax officials will determine if lands previously classified under this act have been reapplied for or have undergone a change in land use [§ 79-A:5 II, IV].

VALUATION

The assessing officials will appraise open space land at valuations based on the current use values established by the current use advisory board [§ 79-A:5 I].

LAND USE CHANGE TAX

Land which has been classified open space land as described above will be subject to a land use change tax when it no longer qualifies for open space assessment. The amount of the tax will be 10 percent of its full and true value in money. This tax is paid in addition to the annual real estate tax [§ 79-A:7 I].

CURRENT USE ADVISORY BOARD

This board is established to function within the tax commission. It will be made up of eleven appointed members: assessing officials, members of the State legislature, commissioner of agriculture, commissioner of the department of resources and economic development, dean of the college of agriculture, and other designated officials. Their duties are to establish a schedule of criteria and values for open space land and to review it yearly. They may also recommend changes in the administration of this act [§ 79-A:3, 4].

Discretionary Easements

ELIGIBILITY

An owner of open space land is eligible to apply for a discretionary easement if: (1) the open space land meets the requirements listed above or (2) the open space land does not meet the requirements, but the owner wants to keep his land in a use consistent with the purposes of the law. The owner will apply to the town planning board or selectmen for a permit to convey a discretionary easement to the town. If the town planning board or the selectmen determine that the proposed use of the land is consistent with open space objectives, then they will recommend that the town acquire the easement [§ 79-A:15, 16].

Having received a permit to convey a discretionary easement, the owner applies to the selectmen or mayor and council to grant an easement to the town not to subdivide, develop, or otherwise change the use of the land to an intensive use inconsistent with the purposes of the law. The easement becomes a burden on the land [§ 79-A:17].

VALUATION

The discretionary easement will include a current use assessment category or it will fix the assessment for the term of the easement. In the latter case, the fixed assessment cannot exceed the highest per acre valuation of any category of open space land established by the current use advisory board. The period of the easement is for at least 10 years [§ 79-A:19].

RELEASE FROM EASEMENT

A landowner may apply to be released from the easement if he or she can demonstrate extreme personal hardship. In order to be released, the owner will have to pay the following amount: if he or she is released during the first half of the term of the easement, 12 percent of the full value assessment; if he or she is released during the second half, 6 percent of the full value assessment [§ 79-A:19 I (a), (b)].

NEW JERSEY

New Jersey amended its constitution in 1963 to enable the legislature to provide for the assessment of agricultural and horticultural land at its value in those uses. The following year the legislature enacted "The Farmland Assessment Act of 1964," a deferred tax law. It was slightly amended in 1970 and 1973.

The constitution enables the legislature to provide that land in agricultural or horticultural use for at least the 2 preceding years and of at least 5 acres size will be assessed according to its value in agriculture [New Jersey Statutes Annotated, Constitution, Art. 8, § 1, paragraph 1].

DEFINITIONS

Land is deemed to be in agricultural use if it is devoted to production for sale of plants and animals useful to man; forages and sod crops; grains and feed crops; dairy animals and dairy products; poultry and poultry products, etc.

Land is deemed to be in horticultural use if it is devoted to production for sale of fruits of all kinds, grapes, nuts, berries, vegetables, and nursery products.

Both of these definitions include land which is in a Federal soil conservation program [§ 54:4-23.3, 54:4-23.4].

ELIGIBILITY

Land is deemed actively devoted to agricultural or horticultural use if the gross sales produced from these uses on the first 5 acres averaged $500 per year during the previous 2 years. For all acreage above 5 acres, an aggregate average gross sales of $5 per acre on farmland and $0.50 per acre on woodland and wetland is required during the previous 2 years, or there must be clear evidence that such anticipated average yearly gross sales will be attained within a reasonable period of time [§ 54:4-23.5]. The owner must apply for special assessment [§ 54:4-23.6]. Eligibility of land will be determined for each tax year separately [§54:4-23.13].

VALUATION

In determining the value of the land, the assessor will consider, in addition to his own experience, knowledge, and judgment, any evidence of agricultural and horticultural capability that is indicated by soil survey data, and the recommendations of any county or State committee established to assist the assessor [§ 54:4-23.7].

STATE FARMLAND EVALUATION ADVISORY COMMITTEE

The members of this committee will annually determine and publish a range of values for each of the classifications of land in agricultural and horticultural use in the various areas of the State. They may use available soil survey data and such other indicators of agricultural capability as they deem pertinent [§ 54:4-23.20].

ROLL-BACK TAXES

Once land use changes, then roll-back taxes will be due for the current and 2 preceding years. In determining the amount of roll-back taxes, the assessor will ascertain: (1) the full and fair value of the land under the valuation standard applicable to other land in the taxing district; (2) the amount of the land assessment by multiplying the full value by the county percentage level; (3) the amount of the additional assessment by subtracting the special assessment from the amount determined above; and (4) the amount of the roll-back tax for that particular tax year by multiplying the amount of the additional assessment by the general property tax rate for that year [§ 54:4-23.8].

NEW MEXICO

New Mexico amended its constitution in 1971 to enable the legislature to enact laws using different methods to tax different classes of property. The constitution now provides that taxes will be uniformly and equally levied in the same class. Different methods may be used to value different kinds of property [New Mexico Statutes, Constitution, Art. VIII, § 1].

The law, which preceded this amendment to the constitution, was enacted in 1967. The law provides for preferential assessment of agricultural land.

DEFINITIONS

Agricultural use of the land means land that is devoted to the production for sale of plants, crops, trees, forest products, or animals useful to man, and land that is in a Federal soil conservation program. Gross sales derived from agricultural use of the land must have averaged $100 per year during the 2-year period preceding the tax year, or there must be clear evidence of anticipated yearly gross sales of at least $100 per year [§ 72-2-14.2]. The land must have been used primarily for agriculture for at least 5 years preceding the tax year [§ 72-2-14.1].

Grazing land means land which is used substantially in the raising of livestock and has been so used for the last 10 years.

ASSESSMENT

The value of such agricultural land is based on the capacity of the land to produce agricultural products [§ 72-2-14.1].

The value of different classes of grazing lands is determined by the State tax commission. Lands of the same carrying capacity are classified and valued equally. The commission is to use the criteria of number of head per section which such land will support reasonably. Value of the lands is to be reduced because of drought or economic conditions, as necessary.

NEW YORK

New York enacted an agricultural value assessment ceiling law in 1971 and amended it in 1972. We have classified part of it as a deferred tax law and part as restrictive agreements. The portion classified as a deferred tax law differs from the typical deferred tax in having a strong element of State and local planning involved. It is based chiefly, though not exclusively, on the establishment of agricultural districts, which may be created by neighboring cooperating farmowners with the approval of local and State authorities. The law also has a section providing for State initiative in forming districts of unique agricultural land. This section is coupled with a State-aid provision whereby the State will make up 50 percent of the revenue lost anually by the local taxing jurisdictions because of State-initiated agricultural districts.

Land not in agricultural districts may be differentially assessed only if the landowner enters into an agreement with the local government to keep the land in agricultural use for 8 years into the future. Hence, this portion of the law constitutes a restrictive agreement.

The New York law also differs from the typical differential assessment law in not permitting classification of real property for assessment and tax purposes. The agricultural value assessment ceiling really constitutes a partial exemption from property taxation for eligible farmland.

DEFINITIONS

Viable agricultural land includes land highly suitable for agricultural production and upon which agriculture will continue to be feasible if real estate taxes, farm use restrictions, and speculative activities are limited to levels such as those in commercial agricultural areas not influenced by neighboring urban development [Agriculture and Markets Law, Art. 25AA, § 301. 1]. Unique and irreplaceable agricultural land includes land which is uniquely suited for the production of high value crops such as fruits, vegetables, and horticultural specialities [§ 301. 2].

Agricultural production means the production for commerical purposes of crops, livestock, and livestock products, but excludes land used to process or retail such products [§ 301. 3].

LANDOWNER INITIATIVE IN CREATION
OF AGRICULTURAL DISTRICTS

Any owner or owners of land who together own a specified minimum of county land may submit a proposal to the county legislative body to create an agricultural district. The proposal will be reviewed by the county planning board, the agricultural districting advisory committee [§ 302], and a public hearing. The proposal will be judged on the basis of viability of farming in the area, extent of other land uses, and patterns of county development. The county legislative body, upon approval of the proposal, may include adjacent viable farmland and exclude nonviable and nonfarm land [§ 302, 303. 1-6]. The proposal is then submitted to the State commissioner of environmental conservation, the agricultural resources commission, and the office of planning services. The first reviews it for consistency with State environmental plans, the second for whether the district consists chiefly of viable agricultural land, and the third for consistency with State comprehensive plans. If these officials approve the proposal, and once the public hearing is concluded, then the agricultural district becomes effective.

Once the agricultural district has been created, it will be reviewed every 8 years. The county legislative body may revise the boundaries or discontinue the agricultural district altogether if it is no longer predominantly viable agricultural land [§ 303. 7-8].

OTHER WAYS TO CREATE AGRICULTURAL DISTRICTS

The commissioner of agriculture may establish an agricultural district for unique and irreplaceable agricultural land [§ 304].

ASSESSMENT OF LAND IN AGRICULTURAL DISTRICTS

A landowner is eligible for agricultural value assessment if: the land is in agricultural production; it is at least 10 acres in size; and for each of the preceding 2 years it produced for sale a gross average sales value of $10,000 or more. The owner must apply yearly [§ 305. 1 a].

DETERMINATION OF AGRICULTURAL VALUE

Agricultural value per acre shall be determined yearly by the State board of equalization and assessment from statistics of the agricultural resources commission and the U.S. Department of Agriculture [§ 305. 1 c].

The assessor will use the average value per acre to determine the amount of assessment for all farmlands eligible for agricultural use assessments. The average value is multiplied by the number of acres used in agricultural production, and a special equalization rate is applied to the result. This final result is the agricultural value ceiling. The value of land in agricultural production which is in excess of the agricultural value ceiling is not subject to real property taxation [§ 305. 1 b, d].

CONVERSION OF LAND IN AGRICULTURAL
DISTRICT TO ANOTHER USE

When land is converted to use other than agricultural production, roll-back taxes will be collected for the past 5 years. Roll-back taxes will be based on the value of the property in excess of the agricultural value ceiling [§ 305. 1 e].

STATE ASSISTANCE TO AGRICULTURAL DISTRICTS

The State will provide assistance to a State-initiated agricultural district equal to one-half the revenue lost because of the special agricultural assessment. The amount of assistance will be reduced by the amount of any roll-back taxes collected that tax year [§ 305. 1 f].

LIMITATION ON LOCAL REGULATION

The statute provides that local government will not unduly restrict or regulate farm structures or practices [§ 305.2]. Any significant exercise of eminent domain in an agricultural district must be approved by the commissioner of environmental conservation [§ 305.4]. The power of a public service district to impose benefit levies or special ad valorem levies on agricultural district land is limited to the one-half acre surrounding the dwelling [§ 305.5].

AGRICULTURAL VALUE ASSESSMENTS OF LAND
NOT IN AGRICULTURAL DISTRICTS

If land is not in an agricultural district, but is in agricultural use, is at least 10 acres in size, and produced the preceding year a gross sales value of $10,000 or more, and if the owner will sign a form committing the land to agricultural use for the next 8 years, then the land is eligible for agricultural value taxation [§ 306. 1]. Commitments must be filed annually. Converting farmland to another use during the 8 years will be considered a breach of commitment and the property owner will pay, in addition to taxes, an amount equal to twice the taxes due on all the committed land in the following year [§ 306. 2].

NORTH CAROLINA

North Carolina enacted a deferred tax law in 1973, effective January 1, 1974. Under this law, individually owned agricultural, horticultural, and forest land is designated as a special class of property for tax purposes.

DEFINITIONS

Agricultural land means land constituting a farm unit, including contiguous woodland and wasteland, which is engaged in the commercial production of crops, plants, or animals under a sound management program [General Statutes of North Carolina, § 105-277.3 (2)].

Horticultural land means land constituting a horticultural unit actively engaged in the commercial production of fruits, vegetables, nursery, or floral products under a sound management program [§ 105-277.3 (3)].

Forest land means land constituting a forest unit actively engaged in the commercial growing of trees under a sound management program [§ 105-277.3 (4)].

A sound management program means a program of production designed to obtain the greatest net return from the land consistent with its conservation and long-term improvement [§ 105-227.3 (5)].

Present use value means the estimated price at which the property would change hands between a willing and financially able buyer and a willing seller under these assumptions: (1) neither of them is compelled to buy or sell, (2) they both know the capability of the property to produce income, and (3) the present use of the property is its highest and best use [§ 105-277.3 (6)].

Individually owned land means land owned by a "natural person" or persons (i.e., not a corporation) [§ 105-227.3 (7)].

ELIGIBILITY

Agricultural and horticultural land is eligible to be designated special class of property if it is individually owned land, is at least 10 acres, and produced for sale agricultural and horticultural products which brought an average gross income of $1,000 per year for the preceding 3 years [§ 105-277.2 (a) (1), (2)].

Forest land is eligible if it is individually owned land and is at least 20 acres [§ 105-277.2 (a) (3)].

Moreover, all three classes of land must be the owner's place of residence or must have been owned by one family for the 7 years preceding [§ 105-277.2 (b) (1), (2)]. Land in one of these classes having a greater value for other uses will be eligible for present use value taxation once the owner applies to the county tax supervisor. He must file application annually [§ 105-277.4(a)]. The tax supervisor will determine if the land meets the qualifying criteria.

VALUATION

If the tax supervisor approves the application, then he will appraise the property according to its present use value. Once a present use value is established, it will continue in effect (except for revisions necessitated by acreage and operations changes) until all property in the county is revalued, at which time a new present use value will be established [§ 105-277.4 (b)].

The tax supervisor is to prepare a schedule of land values, standards, and rules which will result in the appraisal of eligible property at its present use value [§ 105-227.6]. The State property tax commission will insure uniformity among counties by preparing rules, regulations, and standards to be used by county tax officials [§ 105-227.7].

DEFERRED TAXES

The difference between taxes paid on the present use basis and taxes which would have been payable in the absence of such a classification will be a lien on all the taxpayer's real property and so noted in the tax supervisor's records. Should the owner sell the land or should the property lose its eligibility, then deferred taxes for the current year and the preceding 5 years will be due, plus the interest due on unpaid taxes in general [§ 105-360], calculated from the date each year's tax was deferred [§ 105-277.4 (c)]. The owner is responsible for notifying the tax supervisor of a change in ownership or use. If he fails to do so, he is subject to an additional 10 percent penalty on deferred taxes [§ 105-277.5].

NORTH DAKOTA

In 1973, North Dakota enacted a very limited preferential assessment law. Agricultural lands within corporate limits will be classified and valued as agricultural property. Such valuation will be uniform with the assessed value of neighboring agricultural land not within corporate limits [North Dakota Century Code, § 57-02-27].

OHIO

The Ohio legislature amended its constitution in November 1973 to provide for deferred taxation of farmland. The amendment enabled the State legislature to pass laws providing that land devoted exclusively to agricultural use will be valued for real property tax purposes according to its current value for agricultural use. It may also provide for the collection of deferred taxes amounting to the difference between taxes collected according to agricultural use, and taxes which would have been collected had the land been valued like all other land [Amended House Joint Resolution No. 13, 110th General Assembly, Regular Session 1973–1974].

OREGON

Oregon has a deferred tax law. The method for determining deferred taxes depends on whether the farmland is unzoned or zoned agricultural. The law was enacted in 1963 and amended in 1967, 1969, 1971, and 1973.

ELIGIBILITY AND DEFINITIONS

Farm use means the current employment of land, including the land under farm buildings, for the purpose of obtaining a profit in money by raising, harvesting, and selling crops or by the feeding, breeding, management, and sale of livestock, poultry, and other specified uses. It includes land used for preparation and storage of products for market [Oregon Revised Statutes, § 215.203 (2) (a)].

Unless the farm grosses $500 per year for 3 of the 5 preceding calendar years, it will not be considered as being used to make a profit in money. In case of question, the owner must bear burden of proof [§ 215.203 (2) (b)]. If not located in a farm use zone, the farm must have been in farming for the 2 previous years [§ 308.370 (2)]. Furthermore, ". . . the Department of Revenue shall provide by regulation for a more detailed definition of farm use" which is in accordance with the definitions above [§ 308.380 (1)]. All farmland must meet these criteria of farm use in order to be eligible for differential assessment. The procedures for differential assessment depend on whether farm use land is zoned as such or whether it is unzoned.

ZONED FARM USE LAND

The zoning code provides that "Farm Use Zones shall be established only when such zoning is consistent with the overall plan of development of the county" [§ 215.203 (1)] and when the farms meet the definitional criteria above. Land in areas which are zoned for farm use and its compatible uses, if it meets the definition of farm use, is automatically eligible for special assessment and farmers need not apply [§ 308.370 (1)]. The special assessment will continue until the assessor discovers it is no longer being used as farmland or until the owner requests its removal from a farm use zone [1973 Regular Session, Senate Bill 101, New Section 5].

No State agency, city, county, or political subdivision may unreasonably restrict or regulate farm structures or accepted farming practices if the farms are located in an exclusive farm-use zone [1973 Regular Session, Senate Bill 101, New Section 8].

UNZONED FARM USE LAND

On the other hand, farm use land which is not in a farm use zone is eligible upon meeting the definitional criteria of the tax statute. Farmers wanting the special assessment on land not in a farm use zone must apply to the county assessor for it [§ 308.370 (2)].

VALUATION

The Oregon code provides two methods for valuing farm-use land:

1. Farm property is to be assessed for ad valorem purposes based on market data information for comparable uses in bona fide farming. Comparable use is determined when the purchaser meets the "prudent investor for farm use" test [§ 308.345].

2. When comparable sales figures are not available, the assessor may utilize an income approach and the capitalization rate shall be that rate used for appraising nonagricultural commercial land [§ 308.345].

DEFERRED TAXES AND PENALTY

If land in a farm use zone becomes disqualified for special assessment, the assessor will levy a penalty equal to, at most, ten (depending on the number of years the land was so zoned) times the amount by which the taxes would have been larger had it not received the special assessment [1973 Regular Session, Senate Bill 101, New Section 6].

For unzoned agricultural land, the assessor will note on the tax roll the "potential additional tax liability," which would be the difference between taxes collected if there were no differential assessment and taxes collected under differential assessment [ORS, § 308.390, 308.395 (1) (a)].

If unzoned land which has been assessed as farm use land subsequently becomes diverted from farm use or loses its eligibility for the special assessment, the owner must so notify the assessor. Additional taxes will be due in an amount equal to the potential tax liability for up to the previous 10 years plus 6 percent interest calculated from the year taxes were deferred [§ 308.395 (1) (a) (b)].

If the owner should fail to notify the assessor, the assessor will determine the date that notice should have been given. Then he will assess a penalty against the land. The total will equal deferred taxes for up to 10 years, plus 6 percent interest calculated from the year the taxes were deferred, plus the additional taxes which would have been collected had notice been properly given when land use changed, plus interest, plus a 20 percent penalty levied on the latter tax portion (excluding interest) [§ 308.395 (2)].

If unzoned farm use land becomes zoned farm use land, then the potential additional tax liability recorded for unzoned farm use land is cancelled [§ 308.395 (4)]. This, however, does not exempt the land from the laws (and taxes and penalties) governing farm use zones.

OTHER TAXES

With some exceptions, land qualified for farm use assessment will be exempt from the following assessments and levies in these special tax units and districts: sanitary districts, domestic water supply districts, and water and sanitary authorities. The chief exception is that benefit assessments may be imposed on the home site in the parcel of farm use land [1973 Regular Session, Senate Bill 101, New Section 7].

PENNSYLVANIA

Pennsylvania enacted a restrictive agreements law in 1966. In addition, it proposed to amend its constitution in 1973 to permit the general assembly to provide standards and qualifications for forest reserves, agricultural reserves, and land actively devoted to agriculture.

The 1966 statute is based on county and municipal planning and on restrictive covenants with landowners.

DEFINITIONS

Farmland means any tract(s) of land in common ownership of at least 20 acres used to raise livestock or grow crops [Act No. 254 of 1972, § 1 (1)].

Forest land means any tract(s) of land in common ownership of at least 50 acres used to grow timber crops [Public Law 1292, § 1 (2)].

Water supply land means any land used to protect watersheds and the water supply, such as land used to prevent floods and soil erosion, to protect water quality, and to replenish surface and ground water supplies [PL 1292, § 1 (3)].

Open space land means any land including farm, forest, and water supply land, in common ownership, of at least 10 acres, and upon which site coverage by structures, roads, and paved areas does not exceed 3 percent. Open space uses include land, the restriction of which would: (1) conserve natural or scenic resources, such as soils, beaches, streams, wetlands, and tidal marshes; (2) enhance the value of neighboring parks, forests, wildlife preserves, nature reservations, or other public open spaces; (3) increase public recreational opportunities; (4) preserve sites of historic, geologic, or botanic interest; (5) promote orderly urban development; or (6) otherwise preserve open space without structures, roads, or paved areas exceeding the 3 percent site coverage limit [Act No. 254 of 1972, § 1 (4)].

PLANNING REQUIREMENTS

No land will be subject to this act unless designated farm, forest, water supply, or open space land as part of a regional, county, or municipal plan [Act. No. 254 of 1972, § 2].

COVENANTS

Certain classes of counties are authorized to enter into covenants with landowners of farm, forest, water supply, and open space land in order to preserve the land as open space. The county will covenant that the real property tax assessment, for a period of 10 years, will reflect the fair market value of the land as restricted by the covenant [Act No. 254 of 1972, § 3]. The covenant will be renewed annually unless the landowner or the government notify one another otherwise [PL 1292, § 4].

BREACH OF COVENANT

If, during the term of the covenant, the landowner should alter the use of the land, then he shall pay additional taxes. This amount will be equal to the difference between the taxes actually paid and the taxes which would have been paid without the covenant, plus compound interest at 5 percent [PL 1292, § 6].

land, (4) the character of the location, and (5) other applicable factors [§ 10-6-33.1] Capacity to produce agricultural products will be determined by average yields for cropland and average acres per animal unit for grazing land. The averages will be based on a 10-year period [§ 10-6-33.2].

TEXAS

Texas amended its constitution in 1966 to provide for deferred taxes.

DEFINITION

Agricultural use means the raising of livestock, the growing of crops, fruit, flowers, etc., with the further criteria that the land be owned by a "natural person" (i.e., not a corporation), that he be in this business for profit, and that this business be his primary occupation and income source [Texas Statutes Annotated, Constitution, Art. VIII, § 1-d (a)]. The land must have been in agriculture exclusively and continuously for the 3 preceding years [§ 1-d (e)].

ELIGIBILITY

The farmer must apply and file an affidavit for each assessment year he wishes to qualify. The tax assessor shall determine whether the land meets the definitional criteria [§ 1-d (b), (c), (d)].

VALUATION

Qualifying land shall be assessed considering only those factors pertinent to agricultural use.

CHANGE IN LAND USE

Every year, for land designated in agricultural use, the tax assessor will note on the tax rolls what the land would have been valued if it were not in agricultural use. If such land is subsequently put into another use, it will be subject to a tax equal to the difference between its nonagricultural and its agricultural use valuation for the preceding 3 years [§ 1-d (f)].

UTAH

Utah amended its constitution in 1969 to allow the legislature to enact laws pertaining to agricultural use assessment. Accordingly, the legislature enacted the Greenbelt Act in 1969 and amended it in 1973. It provides for deferred taxation.

DEFINITION

Agricultural use means land devoted to the raising of plants and animals useful to man such as: forages and sod crops, grain and feed crops, dairy animals, poultry, livestock, and other specified uses, and land in a cropland retirement program of the State or Federal government [Utah Code Annotated, § 59-5-88].

ELIGIBILITY

The land must have been actively devoted to agricultural use for at least 5 successive years immediately preceding the current tax year. The land must not be less than 5 contiguous acres [§ 59-5-89], but the acreage limitation may be waived by the tax commission if the owner obtains 80 percent of his income from the land [§ 59-5-87 (a)]. The land must have produced an average gross sales of at least $250 per year over the 5 preceding years. The owner must apply [§ 59-5-89 (2), (3) (a)]. Once use assessment has been applied to a tract of land, the owner need not reapply annually. If land use changes, he must notify the county assessor, or be subject to a 100 percent penalty computed on the roll-back taxes [§ 59-5-89 (3) (c)].

VALUATION

The tax assessor in valuing the eligible land will consider only those indicators of value which the land has for agricultural use [§ 59-5-90].

ROLL-BACK TAXES

[If,] once land has been assessed under this act, it loses its eligibility for such assessment because of a change in land use, then it shall be liable for roll-back taxes for up to the previous 5 years. The amount of the roll-back tax is the difference between the taxes paid while assessed under the act and the taxes which would have been paid if not assessed under the act [§ 59-5-91].

FARMLAND EVALUATION ADVISORY COMMITTEE

This committee is established to review the several classifications of land in agricultural use in the various areas of the State and to recommend a range of values for each of the classifications to the State tax commission [§ 59-5-101].

VERMONT

Vermont enacted a differential assessment law in 1969. It is based on the State's control of land use. Two different methods are used: (1) the acquisition by the State of various rights and interests in the land, with the landowner being taxed according to the remaining rights and interests; and (2) contracts between the local government and a farmer to fix the rates of taxation on real and personal property. We have classified it in the restrictive agreements category.

METHOD I

The owner of real property may sell or donate that property or any right or interest therein to a municipality or department of the State if the Vermont planning council approves it [Vermont Statutes Annotated, Title 10, § 6302].

The legislative body of a municipality or department determines the types of rights and interests it will be able to acquire [§ 6303 (b)].

Once the rights and interests in real property have been reconveyed or leased back to a person by a municipality or department, the use of that real property may not be changed unless the appropriate legislative body agrees to the change.

The owner of any remaining right or interest in the land shall be taxed only according to the fair market value of the remaining right or interest [§ 6306 (b)]. The department of taxation, the department acquiring a right or interest in the land, and the owner shall cooperate in determining fair market value [§ 6306 (b)].

Any arrangement for conveyance of rights or interests in real property less than fee simple shall contain a time limitation [§ 6308].

METHOD II

A second portion of the Vermont Code provides that municipal corporations may enter into contracts with farmers and new industrial and commercial establishments to fix and maintain the value and tax of real property for a period not to exceed 10 years [Title 24, § 2741].

VIRGINIA

Virginia amended its constitution in 1970 and enacted a law in 1971 to provide for local government option for deferral of taxes. The law was amended in 1973.

DEFINITIONS

Real estate in agricultural use means real estate devoted to the bona fide production for sale of plants and animals useful to man. Uniform standards will be prescribed by the State commissioner of agriculture and commerce. Land in a Federal soil conservation program may be included [Code of Virginia, § 58-769.5 (a)].

Real estate in horticultural use means real estate devoted to the bona fide production for sale of fruits, vegetables, nursery products, etc. Uniform standards will be prescribed by the commissioner of agriculture and commerce. Land in a Federal soil conservation program may be included [§ 58-769.5 (b)].

Real estate in forest use means land which is planted with trees in such quantity and spaced and maintained to meet the standards of the department of conservation and economic development [§ 58-769.5 (c)].

Real estate in open space use means land used for park or recreational purposes, the conservation of land and other natural resources, floodways, historic or scenic purposes, and for guiding community development. Uniform standards will be prescribed by the director of the commission of outdoor recreation [§ 58-769.5 (d)].

ELIGIBILITY OF CITIES, COUNTIES, AND TOWNS

In order for a city, county, or town to adopt a deferred tax ordinance, it must have adopted a land use plan. The ordinance must provide for at least one of the four classifications of land: agricultural, horticultural, forest, and open space [§ 58-769.6].

ELIGIBILITY OF AGRICULTURAL
OR HORTICULTURAL LAND

Property owners must submit an application for use assessment. A fee may be required at time of application [§ 58-769.8]. The local assessor will determine the eligibility of real estate for those classifications in the local ordinance: agricultural, horticultural, forest, or open space land. He will use the criteria set by the commissioner of agriculture and commerce, the director of the department of conservation and economic development, or the director of the commission of outdoor recreation [§ 58-769.7 (a), § 58-769.12].

Moreover, land in agricultural, horticultural, or open space use must be at least 5 acres in size and forest use land must be at least 20 acres [§ 58-769.7 (b)]. Land which has been valued, assessed, and taxed under such an ordinance will continue to be so treated as long as it remains in its classified use [§ 58-769.8].

VALUATION

The assessor, for land classified as agricultural, horticultural, forest, or open space will consider only those indicators of value which the real estate has for agriculture, horticulture, forest, or open space use. In addition to its own judgment, experience, and knowledge, the assessor will consider evidence of land capability and recommendations of land value made by the State land advisory committee [§ 58-769.9 (a)].

The local commissioner of revenue or assessor will note both the fair market value and the use value in the land book records [§ 58-769.9 (d)].

ROLL-BACK TAXES

If land use changes to a nonqualifying use, then roll-back taxes, equal to the difference between tax based on fair market value and tax based on use value, will be due for up to 5 years preceding the year of the change plus interest of 6 percent per annum [§ 58-769.10].

STATE LAND EVALUATION
ADVISORY COMMITTEE

The committee shall determine and publish a range of suggested values for each U.S. Soil Conservation Service land capability classification. The committee will also submit recommended ranges of values for each locality having an ordinance. The recommendations will be based on productive earning power determined by capitalization of warranted cash rents or by the capitalization of incomes of like real estate in the locality or a reasonable area of the locality [§ 58-769.11].

WASHINGTON

Washington amended its constitution in 1968 to allow current use assessment of farmland, timberland, and other open space lands. A law detailing the methods of differential assessment was enacted in 1970 and amended in 1973. This law includes elements of both deferred tax laws and restrictive agreements, but we have classified it in the latter group.

A second part of the law, enacted in 1971, provides authority for the State to acquire the fee, development rights, or easement to protect and preserve selected open space, farm, and timber land. Taxes will be levied in accordance with the current use of the land.

Agreements

DEFINITIONS

Farm and agricultural land means either (a) land in contiguous ownership of 20 acres or more devoted chiefly to the production of livestock or agricultural commodities for commercial purposes; or (b) any parcel of land 5 acres or more, but less than 20 acres, devoted primarily to agricultural uses which has produced a gross income of at least $100 per acre per year for at least 3 out of the 5 preceding years; or (c) any parcel of land of less than 5 acres devoted primarily to agricultural use which has produced a gross income of $1,000 per year for 3 of the 5 preceding years [Revised Code of Washington, § 84.34.010].

Open space land means (a) land so designated in an official comprehensive land use plan and zoned accordingly, or (b) any land area whose preservation would (1) conserve and enhance natural or scenic resources; (2) protect streams or the water supply; (3) promote the conservation of soils, wetlands, beaches, or tidal marshes; (4) enhance the value to the public of neighboring parks, forests, wildlife preserves, or other open space; (5) enhance recreational opportunities or preserve historic sites; or (6) retain in its natural state land located in an urban area, where the land is at least 5 acres in size and is open to public use [§ 84.34.020 (1)].

Timberland means contiguously owned land of 5 or more acres devoted primarily to the growth and harvest of forest crops [§ 84.34.020 (3)].

ELIGIBILITY

Applications for classification as agricultural land are made to the county assessor who approves or denies them with due regard to all relevant evidence [§ 84.34.030]. Application for open space or timberland classification is made to the county legislative authority which may weigh the benefit to the general welfare from preserving the current use of the land against the loss in tax revenue. It may also consider whether current use fulfills the stated definitions of open space or timber land [Chapter No. 212, Laws of 1973, New Sections 4 and 5].

VALUATION

If the application has been approved, in the case of open space or timber land, the assessor will determine the true and fair value of the land by considering only its current use and excluding any potential uses of the property [§ 84.34.060]. However, in the case of farm and agricultural land, the assessor will determine the value of the land according to the earning or productive capacity (net cash rental) of typical crops grown on comparable lands averaged over at least 5 years and capitalized at a rate of interest charged in long-term loans secured by a mortgage on farm and agricultural land, plus a component for property taxes [Chapter No. 212, Laws of 1973, New Section 10].

RESTRICTIONS ON LAND USE

Once land has been classified under this chapter, it may not be applied to another use for at least 10 years. After 8 years have elapsed, the owner may withdraw his land from classification, effective in 2 years [§ 84.34.070].

ROLL-BACK TAXES

If the landowner withdraws his land from the agricultural, open space, or timber land classification described above, he will be liable for back taxes. The amount will be the difference between the taxes actually collected and taxes which would have been collected had the land not been classified and taxed as agricultural, open space, or timber land, plus interest. The period of the roll-back is the preceding 7 years [§ 84.34.070]. Should land use be changed other than in compliance with the procedures outlined above, then roll-back taxes will be collected, plus interest, plus a penalty of 20 percent of the roll-back taxes. The period of the roll-back is the preceding 7 years [§ 84.34.080].

Land Acquisition

AUTHORITY TO ACQUIRE LAND

Any county, city, town, or metropolitan corporation may acquire the fee or any lesser interest, development rights, easement, covenant, or other contractual right in order to maintain, preserve, and limit the future use of selected open space, farm, and timber land. A city, county, or municipal corporation may acquire the fee to such property in order to convey or lease back such property to its original owner. The development rights to land which has been classified and taxed under the preferential assessment law may specifically be acquired [§ 84.34.210].

WYOMING

Wyoming enacted a preferential assessment law in 1973.

DEFINITION AND ELIGIBILITY

Agricultural land for assessment purposes is land which is presently used to obtain a profit by raising, harvesting, and selling crops or by the feeding, breeding, management, and sale of livestock [Wyoming Statutes, § 39-82 (b) (i)]. Land must have been so used for 2 years previous to agricultural assessment. Agriculture must be its primary use.

ASSESSMENT

Eligible land will be assessed according to its value in its current use, and its capacity in agricultural use. Capacity will be based on average yields of lands of the same classification under normal conditions [§ 39-82 (c)]. However, until 1977, there will be no reduction of assessed valuation of agricultural lands below the levels for 1971 and 1972.

TANGIBLE PERSONAL PROPERTY

Legal Basis for Assessed Value of Selected Classes of Tangible Personal Property, by State: 1975

State[1,2]	Basis[1]
Alabama	Basically, percentages of fair and reasonable value in three classes, same as for realty. . . . Stocks of goods of merchants at not less than 60 percent of fair and reasonable value of the average amount of goods held during 12 months next preceding October 1.
Alaska	Full and true value same as realty. Business inventories may be assessed on basis of average monthly value or value as of January 1.
Arizona	Five classes of personal property, same as realty, with levels at 15 percent to 60 percent of market value (see Supplement D).
Arkansas	20 percent of usual selling price or average value (equivalent as to specified types of personalty, to true and full or actual value).
California	25 percent of fair market value, except aircraft (assessed at fair market value), other minor exceptions.
Colorado	Unless otherwise specified, 30 percent of actual value. Stocks of merchandise at 5 percent of actual value. Livestock at 13 percent of actual value, 1974, thereafter adjusted by length of time owned.

257

State[1,2]	Basis[1]
Connecticut	Not to exceed 100 percent of true and actual or fair market value, but unless otherwise provided, at 70 percent of same, no later than at close of next revaluation.
Florida	Full cash value, same as realty, except inventories, assessed at 25 percent of just valuation.
Georgia	40 percent of fair market value, same as realty. Motor vehicles in dealers' inventories assessed at 75 percent of the assessed value for other motor vehicles.
Idaho	20 percent of market value, same as realty. Personalty coming into state April 1 and after, at fractions of full assessed value.
Illinois	Fair cash value, i.e., 50 percent of actual value, same as realty.
Indiana	33 1/3 percent of market value, same as realty.
Iowa	Actual value, same as realty, effective January 1, 1975 (as to inventory or goods in bulk, market value as such, not retail or unit price).
Kansas	30 percent of fair market value, same as realty.
Louisiana	Actual cash value, same as realty, until 1978. Stocks of merchandise at average inventory value. Plants and storage bases engaged in utilization of waste material assessed at 25 percent of actual value until December 31, 1980.
Maryland	Personal property assessed at full cash value, without allowance for inflation (unlike realty). Stock in trade assessed on basis of lower of cost or market.
Michigan	50 percent of true cash value, same as realty.
Minnesota	Percentages of market value, as specified: Structures on leased public lands, rural areas; tools, implements, and machinery affixed to public utility personalty; leased agricultural realty on leased land— all at 33 1/3 percent. Structures on leased public lands, urban areas and on railroad rights-of-way; all other realty on exempt land; utility systems; billboards, signs, and devices—all 43 percent. Mobile homes; also owner-occupied residences on leased land—classification, as to homestead and value

State[1,2]	Basis[1]
	components, that apply to corresponding residential realty.
Missouri	Effective December 31, 1974, assessed at 33 1/3 percent of true value in money, same as realty.

Montana	Percentages of full cash (or true and full) value, as follows:
	    Agricultural and other tools, implements, and machinery, vehicles of all kinds (except mobile homes), at 20 percent.
	    Livestock, stocks of merchandise of all sorts (including mobile homes held by dealers or distributors) and furniture and fixtures, at 33 1/3 percent. Effective July 1, 1975, however, business inventories are to be assessed at 7 percent of true and full value.

Nebraska	35 percent of actual value, same as realty.
Nevada	35 percent of full cash value, same as realty.
New Jersey	Depreciable personal property used in business assessed at not less than 20 percent of original cost to taxpayer. Other business personal property assessed at 50 percent of its fair value. Personalty of telegraph, telephone and messenger companies assessed on average ratio basis.

New Mexico	Taxable value, set at 33 1/3 percent of full value, same as realty. Personal property inventories, as follows:
	    Compute average acquisition cost on basis of end-of-month amounts.
	    Deduct 85 percent of the average for excise taxes, losses, transportation, other specified expenses.

North Dakota	50 percent of full and true value in money, same as realty.

Ohio	Certain merchants and manufacturers personalty:
	1974 and thereafter—45 percent of true value in money.
	Certain other personalty of merchants:
	    1974—58 percent of true value in money.
	    1975—54 percent of true value in money.
	    1976 and thereafter—50 percent of true value in money.
	Machinery of electric power plants—100 percent of true value in money.
	Tools and machinery used in manufacturing, mining,

State[1,2]	*Basis*[1]
	laundering, dry cleaning, radio and TV broadcasting; specified personalty of rural electric companies, 50 percent of true value in money. Tangible personalty not otherwise classified—50 percent of true value in money.
Oklahoma	35 percent of fair cash value, except stocks of goods assessed on basis of certain average values.
Oregon	100 percent of true cash value, same as realty, except that taxable ships and vessels with Oregon as home port registry are assessed at 40 percent of true cash value; those in intercoastal or foreign trade are assessed at 4 percent of true cash value.
South Carolina	True value in money, same as realty except that property of merchants and manufacturers is assessed at 9 1/2 percent of true value in money since 1972.
South Dakota	60 percent of true and full value in money, same as realty.

Tennessee	Tangible personalty, percentages of actual value:
	  Public utilities—55 percent.
	  Commercial and industrial—30 percent.
	  Other—5 percent.

Utah	30 percent of reasonable fair cash value, same as realty.
Vermont	50 percent of appraisal value (the latter is fair market value), same as realty.
Washington	100 percent of true and fair value in money, same as realty, except as follows: Animals, birds, insects, crops at percentages of true and fair value declining from 75 percent in 1975 to zero in 1983. Equivalent phasing out applicable to business inventories, effective 1974, via 10 percent tax credit, exemption 1983.
West Virginia	True and actual value, but four classes of property, same as realty, each subject to a specified rate limit.
Wisconsin	True cash value, but subject to property tax offsets that reduce tax otherwise paid.

[1] In the following states, and the District of Columbia, the legal basis specified in Supplement D for realty also applies to tangible personalty: District of Columbia, Kentucky, Maine, Massachusetts, Mississippi, New Hampshire, North Carolina, Oregon, Rhode Island, Texas, Virginia, Wyoming.

[2] The following states do not tax tangible personalty: Delaware, Hawaii, New York, Pennsylvania. Several states exempt entire classes of tangible personalty, or portions thereof. For a summary as of 1974, see Supplement N.

Legal Status of Major Types of Tangible Personal Property with Respect to Local General Property Taxation, by State: 1974

State	Commercial and industrial	Agricultural	Household personal property	Motor vehicles
Number of taxing States	47	42	27	22
Alabama	[a]T	[a]T	[a]T	T
Alaska	L	L	[a]L	L
Arizona	[b]T	T	E	E
Arkansas	T	T	T	T
California	[c]T	[a]T	[d]T	E
Colorado	T	T	[d]T	E
Connecticut	[e]T	[a]T	E	T
Delaware	E	E	E	E
District of Columbia	[f]T	[g]E	E	E
Florida	T	T	E	E
Georgia	T	T	[h]T	T
Hawaii	E	E	E	E
Idaho	[i]T	T	[h]T	E
Illinois	T	T	E	[a]T
Indiana	T	T	[d]T	E
Iowa	[j]T	[j]T	E	E
Kansas	T	T	[d]T	T
Kentucky	[k]T	E	E	T
Louisiana	T	E	[a]T	E
Maine	[l]T	[l]T	E	E
Maryland	[a]T	[a]T	[d]L	E
Massachusetts	T	T	E	E
Michigan	T	E	[d]T	E

261

State	Commercial and industrial	Agricultural	Household personal property	Motor vehicles
Minnesota	[m]T	[m]T	[a]L	E
Mississippi	T	E	[a]T	T
Missouri	T	T	[n]T	[n]T
Montana	T	[a]T	[o]E	[p]T
Nebraska	[q]T	[q]T	E	T
Nevada	T	T	T	E
New Hampshire	T	T	E	E
New Jersey	[m]T	T	E	E
New Mexico	[s]T	[s]T	[t]T	E
New York	E	E	E	E
North Carolina	T	[a]T	[a]T	T
North Dakota	[u]T	[u]T	E	[u]T
Ohio	T	T	E	E
Oklahoma	T	T	[a]T	E
Oregon	[v]T	[v]T	[d]T	E
Pennsylvania	E	E	E	E
Rhode Island	[w]T	T	[a]T	T
South Carolina	[x]T	[x]T	E	T
South Dakota	T	T	T	[y]T
Tennessee	[z]T	[a]T	[a]T	T
Texas	T	T	[a]T	T
Utah	[aa]T	[aa]T	E	T
Vermont	T	[bb]T	E	E
Virginia	T	T	L	T
Washington	[cc]T	[cc]T	E	E
West Virginia	T	T	[a]T	T
Wisconsin	[dd]T	[dd]T	E	E
Wyoming	T	T	[a]T	E

Note: T denotes legal taxability; E denotes exemption; L denotes local option; except in Virginia, the option to exempt affected items is exercised in most jurisdictions.

[a] Subject to legal provisions for partial exemptions (in Illinois, as to motor vehicles, only one car is exempt; in New Mexico, as to commercial and industrial, certain inventories are exempt).

[b] Exempt are inventories of a retailer or wholesaler consisting of stocks of materials, unassembled parts, work in progress, and finished products, and inventories of manufacturers engaged in fabrication, production and manufacture, while not consigned or billed to any other party.

[c] Thirty percent of assessed value of business inventories exempt since 1970–71 fiscal year. Legislation in 1972 increased this to 45% for 1973–74 fiscal year and to 50% thereafter.

[d] Taxable only if used in production of income.

[e] Manufacturers' inventories 50% exempt in 1971. Percentage increases by 10% annually to 100%, 1976; other inventories 1/12 exempt in 1971, additional 1/12 exempt annually until totally exempt, 1982. Business equipment and machinery acquired after 1973 assessment date are exempt.

^{f} Business inventories exempt effective July 1, 1974.

^{g} In District of Columbia, not encountered. In Ohio, personalty used in agriculture exempt after 1972.

^{h} Taxable only if held for sale, or commercial use (or for rental in Georgia).

^{i} Inventories exempt 1972 and thereafter; 75% exempt in 1971.

^{j} Effective August 15, 1973, a credit (maximum $2,700) applies against taxable assessed value, specific amount to be set annually, following each year in which growth of state general fund revenue exceeds 5 1/2%. After nine such annual credits, personal property tax to be repealed. All livestock assessed as of January 1, 1973, and thereafter, is exempt.

^{k} Machinery is exempt.

^{l} Inventories, agricultural produce, livestock, forest products, exempt for 1973, subject to tax until April 1, 1976, at 100 per cent valuation. Effective 1973, farm machinery used to produce hay and field crops exempt to an aggregate market value not over $5,000.

^{m} Most personalty now exempt in accordance with 1971 legislation.

^{n} Household personalty exempt effective January 1, 1975. Motor vehicles exempt from property tax, effective January 1, 1975, subject instead at that time to motor vehicle stamp tax.

^{o} Exempt, effective March 30, 1974.

^{p} Motor vehicles constituting the inventory of dealers are exempt.

^{q} Effective January 1, 1973, 12 1/2% of value of certain agricultural, railroad, and business property exempt; an additional 12 1/2% exempt annually until 37 1/2% of value is taxable effective January 1, 1977.

^{r} Inventories exempt.

^{s} Effective 1974, certain inventories are exempt. Taxable inventories assessed in accordance with statutory formula.

^{t} Effective January 1, 1973, assessable at 10% of taxable value of the home, exclusive of land value.

^{u} Most personalty exempt since 1970. Motor vehicles exempt, except mobile homes so assessed.

^{v} Thirty percent of true cash value of inventories exempt in 1973, percentage exempt increases by 10% annually, 100% exempt in 1980. Farm machinery 40% exempt in 1974, fully exempt as of July 1, 1980.

^{w} Manufacturers' inventories exempt.

^{x} Manufacturers' inventories exempt. Certain unused agricultural machinery not included in retailers' taxable inventory. Tax Commission directed to arrive at assessment level of 9 1/2% for merchants' and manufacturers' property, effective May 26, 1972.

^{y} Only unregistered motor vehicles are taxable.

^{z} Tax on inventories held for resale can be applied as a full credit against tax due under the Business Tax of 1971, as amended.

^{aa} Inventories assessable at 8% of reasonable cash value on January 1, 1972; totally exempt January 1, 1973, and thereafter.

^{bb} Machinery and equipment exempt; livestock and poultry subject to legal provision for partial exemption.

^{cc} Effective January 1, 1983, business inventories exempt. Phasing out credits occur annually until then, beginning with a credit of 10% applicable to taxes paid on inventories in 1974, and with the credit subsequently increased by 10% annually. Phasing out via assessment level applies to taxes on animals, birds, insects, and agricultural crops, beginning with a level of 75% applicable for 1975 assessment year.

^{dd} Inventories, manufacturers' materials, finished products and livestock exempt, effective May 1, 1977. A system of annually increasing property tax offsets (related to real property assessment levels) applies until 1977. Manufacturing machinery and certain equipment exempt, effective May 1, 1974.

Index

Administration of property tax:
 how assessors are chosen, 113–122
 how state-level officials are chosen,
  135–148
 how the tax works, 4–5
 how those who judge initial appeals
  are selected, 123–133
 opportunities for appeal, 19–20
 problems, 3–4, 8–11, 16, 23–29,
  40–44
 results of appeals, 20–21
Aged (*see* Elderly persons)
Alabama:
 assessed value of realty: actual level
  of, compared with legal level,
  110
  legal basis for, 103
 tangible personal property: legal
  basis for assessed value of, 257
 taxable status of, 261
 tax officials, how they are chosen:
  assessors, 113
  state-level, 135–136
  those who judge initial appeals,
   123
 tax relief: exemptions, various, 171
  for homeowners and renters,
   150–151
Alaska:
 assessed value of realty: actual level
  of, compared with legal level,
  109
  legal basis for, 103
 tangible personal property: legal
  basis for assessed value of, 257
 taxable status of, 261
 tax officials, how they are chosen:
  assessors, 113
  state-level, 136
  those who judge initial appeals,
   123
 tax relief: exemptions, various,
  171–172
  for farms and open space, 199–200
  for homeowners and renters,
   150–151

Apartments:
 common units of comparison for,
  88
 mind-sets of assessors about, 42–43
 relief for renters in, 64, 150–169,
  171–197
 source of operating data, 96
 tax burden on, as percentage of
  rents, 93–95
 use of gross rent multipliers in
  valuing, 88–90
Appeals:
 example of an actual appeal, 49–63
 expert help for, 45–46
 formal hearings, 19–20
 grounds for, 17–18, 26–35
 informal hearings, 19
 making more effective, 36–44, 47–
  48
 results of, 21
 who judges at state level, 135–148
 who judges initial appeals, 123–133
 who makes most appeals, 21–22
Appraising:
 cost approach, 14, 36–39, 81–84
 income approach, 15, 93–100
 market date approach, 14, 85–91
 methods, 11–16
Arizona:
 assessed value of realty: actual level
  of, compared with legal level,
  110
  legal basis for, 103
 tangible personal property: legal
  basis for assessed value of, 257
 taxable status of, 261
 tax officials, how they are chosen:
  assessors, 113
  state-level, 136
  those who judge initial appeals,
   124
 tax relief: of circuit-breaker type,
  162–163
  exemptions, various, 172
  for homeowners and renters,
   150–151